Lucy Bauer | Eva Holleis | Sue Ireland | Waltraud Wanke

öbv

way2go!

Maturatraining

www.oebv.at

Contents

Reading

Tips and tricks

General tips

- Before reading the text, it's important to study the questions thoroughly. As you read them, highlight important information, such as dates, places or names.
- Consider the title of the text and the picture accompanying it. They help you to quickly get an idea of what the text will be about.
- Highlight the sentences in the text where you've found information on a question so you can check your answers quickly when you're done.
- The questions are always in the order the information occurs in the text. If you have found the answers to questions 1 and 3, for example, the answer to question 2 must be somewhere in between.
- Never leave a question unanswered. Answer every question, even if that means guessing.

Multiple matching (with sentence parts or paragraphs/texts) (MM)

- Cross out the options you've used. The task gets easier the more parts you've matched correctly.
- If you're asked to match parts of sentences, pay attention to their grammatical structure as well as the content. Not all beginnings will be possible matches for all endings.
- Only fill in answers you're sure of. Picking a wrong option could lead to another mistake elsewhere. If you're unsure, write down all the possible options and decide at the end.

Multiple choice (MC)

- There is always only one correct answer to each question.
- If you aren't sure about the answer to a question, eliminate the options you know are wrong and then take a guess.

True/False/Justification (T/F/J)

- The text will always give you information on each statement. A statement is considered 'false' if the text gives you different information on it.
- You must use the first four words of the sentence that gives you the information. This one sentence should include all the information necessary to answer the question.
- A new sentence starts after a full stop. A word is everything between two spaces.
- Justify your answer for both true and false statements.

Four-word sentence completion/Four-word answers (4W)

- If the text gives you more than one possible answer, write down only one of them. Never write answers like "he likes food/cars".
- Words or phrases as you find them in the text will not always function properly as answers or sentence completions, you might have to rephrase them.
- Never write more than four words. No matter how good your answer is, it will still be wrong.
- Don't worry too much about spelling or grammar, your answer only has to be clear.

You can find the answer key to all tasks online.
Go to www.oebv.at and type in this code: g55m3g.

Multiple matching (sentence parts)

1 Read the text about one aspect of tourism today. Some parts are missing. Choose the correct part (A–M) for each gap (1–10). There are two extra parts that you should not use. Write your answers in the boxes provided. The first one (0) has been done for you.

When does tourism become unethical?

As humans, we move. We travel; we always have. **(0)** ______ ; we migrated from Africa thousands of years ago, walking out of the savannah to the rest of the world. **(1)** ______ of the Western world's fastest-growing industries. We leave home to climb mountains and trek through rainforests, to dance in Cuba, swim the Hellespont, barter in a souk or lie on a beach.

In his book *The Art of Travel*, the philosopher Alain de Botton contemplates the underlying reasons for travel. **(2)** ______ , he says, for he believes that "there are inner transitions we can't properly cement without a change of locations." Change is also a key motivator in the mind of the late travel writer Bruce Chatwin. "Change of fashion, food, love and landscape," he wrote. "We need them as the air we breathe." **(3)** ______ , for pleasure, for enlightenment; to ease the tedium of daily routine and satisfy the imaginings of curious minds. We travel to shake up our souls and to placate an atavistic restlessness within us. Ernesto Che Guevara thought that we simply "travel just to travel."

(4) ______ ; travellers now have the opportunity to roam further, higher and wilder than before. This means that they risk coming into contact with remote indigenous communities, for the world's remote corners – the green depths of the Amazon basin or the highlands of West Papua – are often the lands and homes of tribal peoples. Their homelands sustain them physically and spiritually, and they understand them intimately. The Yanomami people who live deep in the Brazilian Amazon know the streams and rapids of the rainforest in the same way the Inuit understand the sea-ice of the Canadian Arctic. And this is where the problems with this kind of travel start because it can simply be dangerous for both tourists and little-contacted tribal peoples to meet. **(5)** ______ and tourists can transmit infectious diseases to which little-contacted peoples have no immunity.

Curiosity in other cultures is natural. **(6)** ______ by travelling with ethically-run eco-tourism companies. But the line between ethical and non-ethical is extremely fine. So where does it lie?

(7) ______ visiting tribal peoples who have been in routine contact with outsiders for some time. But as natural social sensitivity and respect would dictate, this only applies to tribal peoples who are happy to receive visitors, have proper control over where the tourists go and what they do in their communities, and receive a fair share of the profits. More often than not, however, only the tiniest proportion of tourism's profits – if any – go to recompensing the tribe; there are very few enterprises that genuinely bring benefits. (8) ______ and involve small, well-managed and low-impact tours.

(9) ______ very carefully about the long-term effects on tribal peoples, not the fleeting thrill of the experience or the glory of the story once back home. (10) ______ in international law, and should be respected regardless of whether the national government applies the law or not. So when in tribal lands, tourists should behave as they would on any other private property. It goes – or should go – without saying that tribal peoples have the same basic human rights as everyone else, which must be upheld.

A	Adventure travel is tourism's recent offspring
B	These are not very environmentally friendly
C	To gain perspective is one
D	Journeying is hard-wired in the human psyche
E	These are often run by tribal peoples themselves
F	Tribes are likely to react with hostility towards outsiders
G	For example, tribal peoples' ownership of the lands they use and occupy is recognised
H	In principle, there is little harm in tourists
I	In fact, ethical tourist companies operating in remote regions have rights and even
J	So we travel for knowledge
K	Tourists can, at times, even help
L	Travellers thinking of visiting tribal areas need to think
M	Today, tourism is still one

0	1	2	3	4	5	6	7	8	9	10
D										

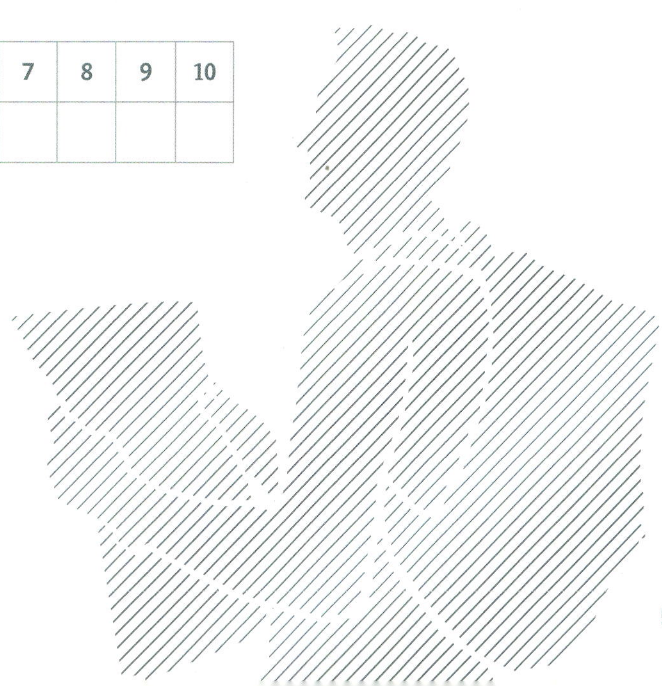

Multiple matching (texts)

2 **Read the extracts from Chris's list of favourite classic science fiction stories. Choose the correct texts (A–F) for each statement (1–11). You can use a text more than once. Write your answers in the boxes provided. The first one (0) has been done for you.**

Great sci-fi stories

A

I like character-driven stories, light-hearted humor and a twist that sneaks up on you, and science fiction author William Tenn delivered truly wicked humor and characterization in *Time in Advance*. It is the story of a man who's about to commit a lethal crime. Far from being a dark story of a vicious criminal secretly planning a covert murder, Tenn's tale takes a light approach. In this world, society views the crime as perfectly legal, if something of a novelty. The hero is aiming to commit a vile crime, and not only is nobody about to stop him, his criminal intentions make him a celebrity.

B

Nightfall, published first in *Astounding Science Fiction* in 1941, is a classic science fiction short story, no doubt about it. Asimov made it into a novel, too. I haven't read the novel. But this story really is mind-blowing. Devastating. But in a good way. It's not the writing. *Nightfall* is easy and enjoyable to read. But typical of Isaac Asimov, the writing is not as tight as it could be, and the dialogue wanders a bit. It's a tad long for what it is. The characters, though well-defined, lack that spark that would make them truly likable. But all that doesn't matter. Because the ending is really unexpected – or it was, for me – and has a mind-blowing effect.

C

Me – I'm a sucker for time travel. The kind of time travel many critics scoff at as clichéd. Time travel in which the attempt to break the second law of thermodynamics and betray nature's linear preference causes a shocking paradox. Time travel used as a vehicle to teach bad people the good lesson that enterprise driven by self-serving greed has a price. It's trite. It's old-fashioned. But gee. That's a *good story*. And that's what's missing from today's fiction. The 1943 piece *The Time Locker* is creative, and funny, and it's one of the very best.

D

Though the story's disturbing premise – that a servile android-robot could turn on its human superiors and commit murder – was probably radical at the time, without Bester's way with words, *Fondly Fahrenheit* wouldn't have become the classic science fiction short story that it is today, still cited as one of the best sci-fi stories ever.

E

By His Bootstraps is another time travel story. I didn't like the main character. Heinlein's characters just don't do it for me. But at least this story is about a character, and not a society that doesn't seem real (which is one of my complaints about Heinlein's stories). Reading the story is pure fun. The paradoxical logic was terribly clever. And as the story unfolded, it became obvious that it was perhaps the best time travel story I'd ever read. As a bonus, it's re-readable, despite the fact that the ending is not exactly forgettable. It's like re-reading an Agatha Christie novel. You remember whodunnit, but you want to see how you were tricked.

F

Pipeline to Pluto is a highly detailed and convincing tale of space travel. The story describes a prosaic world of blue-collar transportation – freight, in fact. Like much Golden Age science fiction, the story, told through fast-paced narrative and dialogue, isn't concerned with conveying a political viewpoint or defending a special interest group. It's concerned with ideas: the concepts, possibilities, and ironies of a newly technological world unfolding for human beings possessed of universal flaws and compromised value systems.

According to Chris, this story/these stories ...

later appeared in a different form.	0	
has something in common with another author's work.	1	
shows wrongdoing being regarded as acceptable behaviour.	2	
became famous mainly due to the author's good use of language.	3	
has a quality rarely to be found in contemporary works of this kind.	4	
is about advanced technology getting out of control.	5	
is more enjoyable than others written by the same author.	6	
develop in a way that is satisfyingly surprising.	7	8
deals with concepts that are often found in classic science fiction stories.	9	
fail to satisfy him completely in some respects.	10	11

0	1	2	3	4	5	6	7	8	9	10	11
B											

Four-word answers

3 Read the text about the early years of flight. Answer the questions (1–8) using a maximum of 4 words. Write your answers in the spaces provided. The first one (0) has been done for you.

How the plane got off the ground

The honor is indisputably theirs: Wilbur and Orville Wright made the first powered, sustained, controlled, heavier-than-air flights at Kill Devil Hills, North Carolina on December 17, 1903.

But even though they had succeeded, the Wrights recognized that they had a considerable distance to go before they could claim to have developed a practical flying machine. So they continued their work in a Dayton cow pasture in 1904 and 1905. By the fall of 1905, they had transformed the marginal success of 1903 into the reality of a practical airplane capable of traveling many miles through the air and remaining aloft for more than an hour at a time. The Wrights worried about being copied, though. Unwilling to unveil their creation without the protection of a patent and a signed sales contract, the brothers remained on the ground for the next two and a half years as they attempted to market their invention.

So it was that as 1908 dawned, almost no one realized that the age of winged flight had been under way for more than four years. That was about to change. With contracts for the sale of airplanes to a French syndicate and the U.S. Army finally in hand, the Wrights were ready to take to the air once again that spring. They returned to the Kill Devil Hills with a rebuilt version of their 1905 airplane – now modified with upright seating and controls, and a second seat for a passenger. On May 14, 1908, Wilbur and Orville alternated taking Charles Furnas, one of their mechanics, up as the world's first airplane passenger.

The excitement peaked on August 8, 1908, when Wilbur Wright made his first flight in public at the Hunaudières race course, five miles south of Le Mans, France. Over the next several weeks he made headlines around the world with one stunning flight after another – demonstrating once and for all that the Wrights' claim to priority in the invention of the airplane was true (there had been skeptics), and that their airplanes were capable of tight turns and a degree of control impossible with other machines.

Orville Wright joined his brother in the limelight on September 3, 1908, when he made his first public flight at Fort Myer. Like Wilbur, he continued to fly over the next two weeks, carrying passengers and meeting criteria established by the Army for the purchase of an airplane. Tragedy struck on September 17, when Orville crashed at Fort Myer while flying with Selfridge, who became the first person to die in a powered airplane crash. Orville recovered, but lived with the pain resulting from the accident for the rest of his life.

The momentous year was far from over. On October 16, the American Samuel Franklin Cowdery (aka S.F. Cody) made the first flight in Great Britain. Once Orville Wright was back on his feet, he and his sister Katharine joined their brother in Europe. The three Wrights were now the toast of the continent. Crowned heads, political leaders, captains of industry and ordinary folk traveled to witness the miracle of flight. Wilbur capped this extraordinary year with a flight of more than 76 miles in 2 hours 18 minutes $33\frac{3}{5}$ths seconds on December 31, which earned him the Michelin Cup and a 20,000-franc cash prize for the best flight of 1908.

By year's end, no skeptic doubted that the age of flight had arrived, and that the Wrights were leading the way.

0	What did the Wrights manage to do between 1903 and 1905?	develop a practical plane
1	Towards the end of 1905, what did the Wrights suspect might happen if they continued flying?	
2	Why did the Wrights feel prepared to fly in 1908?	
3	What made it possible for Furnas to fly with Wilbur in the 1908 plane?	
4	Why was the event near Le Mans so special?	
5	In what way were the Wrights' planes superior to other planes? (Give one answer.)	
6	What was the important thing about Orville's flights as far as one particular institution was concerned?	
7	Why did people of all kinds come together in the autumn of 1908?	
8	What was the outcome of Wilbur's achievement at the end of 1908? (Give one answer.)	

Four-word sentence completion

4 **Read the text about dressing for the office. Complete the sentences (1–9) using a maximum of four words. Write your answers in the spaces provided. The first one (0) has been done for you.**

What to wear to work

Summer's arrival in the northern hemisphere brings with it a dilemma that plagues every office worker. What does a casual dress code mean in practice? The happy medium between looking like Kim Kardashian or Hagrid the giant is hard to pin down.

Goldman Sachs has just implemented a "flexible dress code", although the executive memo noted that "casual dress is not appropriate every day." Besuited corporate clients might not take kindly to investment-banking advice offered by someone wearing a tank top and ripped jeans.

For men, the move to casual dress seems entirely positive. Few people will mourn the demise of the tie, a functionally useless garment that constricted male necks for a century. The tie's origins date back to the 17th century, when mercenaries hired by Louis XIII of France wore a form of cravat. The modern version of the tie emerged in the 1920s and was popularised by Britain's Edward VIII. It became standard office wear for the next six decades. In the 1990s ties started to go out of fashion because technology titans and hedge-fund managers refused to wear them – and were rich enough to ignore social convention. Once, when Mark Zuckerberg, the founder of Facebook, was to meet a venture capitalist, he turned up wearing pyjamas.

The jacket, by contrast, is a much more useful garment, replete with pockets to house wallets, spectacle cases and travel passes (or, these days, mobile phones). So the default work garb for men, when meeting clients, is jacket, open-necked shirt and dark trousers (denim excluded). On days without meetings, men can slob out in T-shirts (though not too garish) and jeans, and no one will think the worse of them. Arriving in shorts or without socks is another matter entirely. But dressing in the morning is quick and easy. Steve Jobs was famous for wearing the same outfit – black polo neck, jeans and trainers – every day.

Women's workwear seems to have become less formal over time. A survey by Euromonitor found that sales of women's suits fell by 77% in America between 2007 and 2016. But many women worry that they will be judged as unprofessional (unlike their male colleagues) if their clothes are deemed to be too scruffy, or too revealing. It can also be hard choosing clothes that are suitable for both indoors and out.

Air-conditioning systems in offices are often designed to suit the male metabolic rate, which can cope with colder temperatures than the female body. The result may be that women have to bring an extra layer to wear in the building.

As for formal meetings, while men have abandoned the tie, many women feel obliged to wear high heels. These give some women a sense of empowerment and femininity (not to mention extra height). But in health terms, heels can seem like the Western equivalent of the ancient Chinese practice of foot-binding: bad for women's feet, ankles and backs and designed to limit their mobility. Britain's parliament held a debate after a woman was sent home from her job as a receptionist for refusing to wear high heels (it was inconclusive).

Companies understandably want workers who deal with the public to look respectable. Workers shouldn't wear clothes that wouldn't be appropriate if visiting a prudish grandmother or a child's teacher. And yet no one should be expected to turn up at the office as if dressed for a wedding. The most important item to bring to work is a dose of common sense.

0	It is difficult to know what kind of outfit is acceptable for work when there is _____ .	*a casual dress code*
1	Despite becoming more tolerant, one firm still believes that an informal outfit is _____ .	
2	Regarding clothes serving a practical purpose, the author believes that the tie is _____ .	
3	Something similar to a tie first appeared in _____ .	
4	Ties began losing popularity when influential businessmen stopped caring about _____ .	
5	Although sometimes permitted, when dealing with the public, one must avoid wearing _____ . (Give one answer.)	
6	Over a certain period, the U.S. saw a significant decrease in purchases of _____ .	
7	Female office workers find it difficult to judge how much they need to wear due to _____ .	
8	One particular fashion is similar to an old custom in that it restricts the wearer's ability to _____ .	
9	In the author's opinion, a suitable office outfit would also always be suitable for meeting _____ . (Give one answer.)	

True/False/Justification

5 Read the text about what gyms were like in the past. First decide whether the statements (1–10) are true (T) or false (F) and put a cross (x) in the correct box. Then identify the sentence in the text which supports your decision. Write the first four words of this sentence in the space provided. There may be more than one correct answer; write down one only. The first one (0) has been done for you.

The origins of the gym

Today people nurture an obsession with a so-called wellness lifestyle that puts a young, toned body at the top of the priority list. Gluten-free diets, green smoothies, yoga, and SoulCycle – you name it!

However, if we go back in time, we'll see that even our ancestors liked to hit the gym, though sometimes for different reasons than obtaining the perfect beach body. According to Eric Chaline, the author of *The Temple of Perfection: A History of the Gym*, throughout history, the gym has been "a place that assembled the artistic and the political, the enlightened and the reactionary, touching on many areas of life, culture, and society." As a tribute to the gods, the ancient Greeks used to go to the gym naked, a notion integrated into the semantics of the word "gymnasium", which translates as "school for naked exercise" and, reportedly, resembled an outdoor athletic field.

Narcissus and his fellow ancient Greeks admired the naked male body, which they perfected by practicing competitive sports or exercising in gyms. The Romans, on the other hand, were a bit skeptical of obsessing over the body and its physical pleasures. In the Middle Ages, the body was feared as a well-spring of immoral pleasures that had to be kept in the dark, and those who gloried in their physiques received a tongue lashing. When the Renaissance commenced, artists brought the nude back in the game, combining it with pagan elements and Christian motifs. The result? Botticelli's *Birth of Venus* and Michelangelo's *David*, masterpieces that praised physical beauty as a symbol of divinity. Nowadays, it can be said that people have returned to the classical Greek model of body observance, making gyms socially necessary venues where people go to meet with friends or even find someone to date.

The concept of a place established exclusively for exercise was actually launched in the 16th century, when Renaissance artists and physicians recognized the benefits of exercise: it provided an attractive figure and promoted a balance in health. Despite this, the idea that body shape could be changed wasn't present until humanity's attitude toward embodiment was altered during the Enlightenment. This period underlined the importance of physical education and the enjoyment of one's own body.

The gym saga continues with Napoleon's defeat of Prussia, which provoked Friedrich Jahn to create the *turnplatz*, the first institution of physical exercise that would train the united citizen army of Germany. The *turnplatz* was an open-air venue that set the foundations for artistic gymnastics, equipped with rings, high bars, ladders, climbing masts and other facilities for various field sports. The place was open to all the social classes, and its practitioners were called *turner*. Two of Jahn's students who emigrated to America during the 1820s set up the first collegiate gymnasium, but it was soon closed.

During the 19th century, and the period of rapid industrialization and urbanization of Western Europe, the affluent Victorians with time for leisure paid much attention to physical self-improvement as a sign of good life quality. The world's first commercial gym was Hippolyte Triat's Grand Gymnase, established in 1849 in France. The first chain of branded gyms, Shadow's Institutes of Physical Culture, opened in the United Kingdom in 1897.

As time went by, Europe's middle class manifested a growing demand for physical fitness, which was once maintained primarily by the members of the upper social class. Both Shadow and Triat used this notion to popularize the "Grecian ideal" of a healthy, attractive body, promoting it with still photography as well as providing standardized equipment for their gyms. Shadow was quite influential in America, which he toured with his carefully selected representatives of health, fitness and weight training.

By the end of the 19th century, there were elite collegiate gyms and even exclusive leisure centers for exercising.

	Statements	T	F	First four words
0	The gym has always attracted a wide variety of people.	☒	☐	According to Eric Chaline
1	In early times, men exercised without clothing in order to compare their bodies to others'.	☐	☐	
2	The human body was considered to be a source of sin during one particular period.	☐	☐	
3	Reasons for going to the gym are currently quite different from what they were at any other time in the past.	☐	☐	
4	The idea that being physically active can prevent medical problems is a modern one.	☐	☐	
5	With new perceptions of the human body, people began to realise that you had to accept your body the way it was.	☐	☐	
6	One gym facility was created for a purpose beyond merely exercising.	☐	☐	
7	People from different kinds of backgrounds went to the *turnplatz*.	☐	☐	
8	People who could afford to take a break from work took an interest in their personal sense of well-being.	☐	☐	
9	The first gym set up with the purpose of making money was one of a set.	☐	☐	
10	Images of physical perfection were included in advertising for gyms.	☐	☐	

Multiple choice

6 **Read the text about learning languages. Then choose the correct answer (A, B, C or D) for questions 1–6. Put a cross (x) in the correct box. The first one (0) has been done for you.**

In other words

Scientists mostly agree that children are better language learners, but do not know why. Some posit biological factors. Is it because young brains have an extreme kind of plasticity? Or, as Steven Pinker, a Harvard psychologist, argues, an instinct for language-learning specifically, which fades as the brain ages and (in evolutionary terms) is no longer needed? Others think children have special environments and incentives, not more conducive brains. They have a strong motivation to communicate with caregivers and intimate peers and are not afraid of making mistakes in the way adults are.

Some believe any "critical period" may only apply to the sounds of a foreign tongue. Adults struggle with accents. But grammar is different, and some researchers have reckoned that adults, with their greater reasoning powers, are not really at a disadvantage relative to children. One study found that when adults and children are exposed to the same teaching materials for a new language for several months, the adults actually do better. Most such research has had to rely on small numbers of subjects, given the difficulty of recruiting them; it is hard to know how meaningful the results are.

Now a large new study led by Joshua Hartshorne of Boston College has confirmed the critical period hypothesis. The study ingeniously recruited 670,000 online test-takers by framing the exercise as a quiz that would guess the participants' native language or dialect. This made it a viral hit. The real point was to test English-learners' knowledge of tricky bits of grammar, and to see how this correlates with the age at which their studies began.

Do younger beginners do better because their earlier start gave them more learning time, or because they learned faster in early years? It can be hard to tease apart these two questions. But testing a huge amount of data against a number of possible learning curves allowed Mr Hartshorne to do precisely that. Many previous researchers had posited a

drop-off at around puberty. The new study found it to be rather later, just after 17.

Despite that later cut-off, learners must begin at around ten if they are to get to near-native fluency. If they start at, say, 14, they cannot accumulate enough expertise in the critical period. Unfortunately, 14 or so is precisely when many students, especially in America, are first introduced to a new language. (Even worse, this is an age when children are acutely sensitive to embarrassment in front of peers.)

Children who start at five don't do noticeably better than those who start at ten over their lifetimes. But there is still reason to begin in the first years of school. Because mastery takes a long time – perhaps 30 years until improvement ceases –, those who begin at five and are obliged to read and write English at university will by then have made much more progress than those who took the plunge at ten, even if their level is roughly the same by 40.

The existence of the critical period is not a reason for anyone 11 or older to give up. Some people remain excellent language students into adulthood. And Mr Hartshorne tested some truly subtle features of grammar that take years to master. A language learned even to a lower level can still be extraordinarily useful at work or enjoyable while travelling.

But for policymakers, the implication is clear. Earlier is better. Many bureaucrats can hardly see past reading and maths. That is a mistake for many reasons. This study demonstrates one of them.

0 Some experts believe youngsters are good at language learning because they

- A use the language more correctly. ☐
- B are better at remembering things than adults. ☐
- C have an urgent need to learn. ☒
- D can reproduce sounds more accurately than adults. ☐

1 When it comes to learning the structures of a language,

- A youngsters are generally less successful than older learners. ☐
- B older learners have problems learning them without textbooks. ☐
- C youngsters have problems learning them from textbooks. ☐
- D older learners can be just as successful as youngsters. ☐

2 Mr Hartshorne's study was an improvement on previous studies in that

- A a very large number of people participated. ☐
- B it proved exactly what experts had always suspected. ☐
- C the participants were invited to take part in a game. ☐
- D it was carried out over a meaningful time span. ☐

3 Mr Hartshorne's research aimed to find out if there was a connection between

- A the participants' mother tongues and their grammar competence. ☐
- B the age of the participants and their grammar competence. ☐
- C learners' grammar competence and when they started writing in the language. ☐
- D learners' grammar competence and when they started learning the language. ☐

4 To be successful at language learning, U.S. students

- A need to work harder on improving their skills. ☐
- B should begin studying languages earlier than most currently do. ☐
- C need to begin studying languages before the age of ten. ☐
- D should be encouraged to be more self-confident. ☐

5 The advantage for those who start learning languages very early on is that they

- A end up with much better language skills later in life. ☐
- B benefit more from the critical period for effective learning. ☐
- C will do well at English-speaking universities. ☐
- D will continue to get better at languages longer than others. ☐

6 In the author's opinion, Mr Hartshorne's research shows that

- A government officials often only have very basic skills nowadays. ☐
- B the age they start learning a language does not matter for those with a talent. ☐
- C some people in important positions need to reconsider their priorities. ☐
- D older people can only learn a language well enough to use it on holiday. ☐

Listening

Tips and tricks

General tips

- Before listening, read the task carefully, including the title and picture. Start thinking about what the recording will deal with. If you know what to expect, it will be much easier for you to understand the content.
- Read the items (options, questions, sentence parts, etc.) carefully. Brainstorm different ways of expressing the same ideas. The language used in the recording will be different from the language in the items.
- Highlight relevant keywords and phrases in the questions or options. Pay special attention to expressions like 'the biggest problem', 'at first he thought' or 'it puts the main focus on'. Expressions like these mean that you will hear about more than one idea and have to choose the correct one.
- Use the first time you listen to the recording to choose an answer to every question in a preliminary way. Use the second time to either confirm or change your choices.
- After listening for the first time, you don't have to be sure about each answer yet. But you should have a good idea of the structure of the recording and know when you need to listen most closely.

Multiple matching (sentence parts or statements to speakers) (MM)

- If you're asked to match parts of sentences, pay attention to their grammatical structure as well as the content. Not all beginnings will be possible matches for all endings. You could try writing the letters of possible matches next to the first halves of the sentences before you listen.
- If you have to match speakers to statements, check the task carefully to see how many statements each speaker gets. This might vary from speaker to speaker.

Multiple choice (MC)

- You may hear expressions or ideas from all four options, but only one answer is correct.
- Try crossing out options you've heard that are wrong.
- If you still aren't sure about the answer to a question after listening for the second time, eliminate the options you know are wrong and then take a guess.

Four-word sentence completion/Four-word answers (4W)

- Think about possible answers when reading the task. Does the question ask for a name or a number? Does the sentence need an object, a person or an activity to complete it?
- If the audio gives you more than one possible answer, write in only one of them. Never write answers like "he likes food/cars".
- Words or phrases as you find them in the audio will not always function as answers or sentence completions, you might have to rephrase them.
- Never write more than four words. No matter how good your answer is, it will still be wrong.
- Don't worry too much about spelling or grammar, your answer only has to be clear.

p7fp8s **Go to www.oebv.at and type in the code p7fp8s to access the audio files you need for the following listening tasks. If you need the key and the transcripts, use this code: g55m3g.**

Multiple matching (sentence halves)

p7fp8s

1 You are going to listen to a radio feature about *TaskRabbit*, an online job marketplace. First you will have 45 seconds to study the task below, then you will hear the recording twice. While listening, match the beginnings of the sentences (1–8) with the sentence endings (A–K). There are two extra sentence endings that you should not use. Write your answers in the spaces provided. The first one (0) has been done for you.

After the second listening, you will have 45 seconds to check your answers.

Taskers

0	*TaskRabbit* is designed to help people to ____ .	B
1	*TaskRabbit* claims to be able to ____ .	
2	Before joining *TaskRabbit*, Juan Diego used to ____ .	
3	Juan Diego expects to ____ .	
4	The idea for *TaskRabbit* originated after a couple had forgotten to ____ .	
5	Allie liked *TaskRabbit* because it isn't necessary to ____ .	
6	If Allie's clients give her good feedback, she hopes to ____ .	
7	Busy working mothers use *TaskRabbit* to ____ .	
8	Clients can be confident that taskers will ____ .	

A	be honest and reliable
B	hire occasional extra assistance
C	take a small percentage
D	catch up with jobs that need doing
E	supply any service a client might request
F	work in the hospitality industry
G	earn a minimum amount every month
H	buy an important item
I	work in other cities
J	sign up for regular hours
K	charge more per hour

Multiple choice

p7fp8s

2 **You are going to listen to a recording about a short career in sports. First you will have 45 seconds to study the task below, then you will hear the recording twice. While listening, choose the correct answer (A, B, C or D) for each question (1–8). Put a cross (☒) in the correct box. The first one (0) has been done for you.**

After the second listening, you will have 45 seconds to check your answers.

A former footballer

0 The football match on 23rd January was important for Cambridge fans because

A their opponents were in the top division. ☒
B both teams were in the Premier League. ☐
C it was the first match of the season. ☐
D they had lost several games previously. ☐

1 Maiorana had to leave the Cambridge United Junior Team when

A he reached the upper age limit. ☐
B his father asked him to join the family business. ☐
C he was told he didn't have the build for a footballer. ☐
D he had an offer from a better local team. ☐

2 Maiorana thought the call from Manchester United was a joke because

A the club contacted him at the weekend. ☐
B it was not long since the scout had seen him. ☐
C he was expected for training at such short notice. ☐
D he'd only played half a season with Histon. ☐

3 When he started playing in the First Team, Maiorana felt

A intimidated by his famous teammates. ☐
B homesick for his old club. ☐
C nervous about appearing on television. ☐
D unprepared for the large crowds. ☐

4 The press said that Maiorana

A had a great future.

B could be a media star.

C should play for England.

D was the best player ever.

5 After his knee operation, Maiorana

A gave up hope of doing any sport again.

B knew he was too old to recover completely.

C took up a completely new profession.

D attempted to resume his playing career.

6 Maiorana dealt with his new situation by

A getting support from former colleagues.

B trying to avoid any contact with football.

C helping young players where he lived.

D immersing himself in his upholstery work.

7 Maiorana no longer felt regretful about the past once

A he met his wife and got married.

B his second child was born.

C he got in touch with old friends on social media.

D he realised he could be proud of his achievements.

8 Maiorana didn't attend the big match in Cambridge because he

A had given his ticket to his son.

B didn't want to see Cambridge beaten.

C wanted to let other people have the opportunity.

D thought it would bring back old memories.

Multiple matching (speakers)

p7fp8s

3 You are going to listen to four young people from around the world talking about their response to climate change. First you will have 45 seconds to study the task below, then you will hear the recording twice. While listening, match the speakers with their statements (A–L). There are two extra statements that you should not use. Write your answers in the boxes provided. The first one (0) has been done for you.

After the second listening, you will have 45 seconds to check your answers.

Saving the planet

Speaker 1 – Brian	0	1	
Speaker 2 – Ella	2	3	
Speaker 3 – Travis	4	5	6
Speaker 4 – Ava	7	8	9

A	I was inspired by a news item I read online.
B	I want all power to come from sustainable sources in the future.
C	Many people in my locality are unaware of the situation.
D	Ocean pollution first alerted me to the environmental crisis.
E	The government wants to profit from the environment rather than protect it.
F	My country is experiencing unpredictable extremes of weather.
G	Getting an interview with a politician was a positive step for us.
H	My latest project has the support of some people from the world of entertainment.
I	Public events have become more environmentally-friendly as a result of my action.
J	Time is running out for people to rescue the situation.
K	Young voices attract attention and have a powerful impact.
L	I started choosing green alternatives at an early age.

0	1	2	3	4	5	6	7	8	9
F									

Four-word answers

p7fp8s

4 **You are going to listen to an interview about a plan for Glencrombie Estate in the Scottish countryside. First you will have 45 seconds to study the task below, then you will hear the recording twice. While listening, answer the questions (1–8) using a maximum of four words. Write your answers in the spaces provided. The first one (0) has been done for you.**

After the second listening, you will have 45 seconds to check your answers.

Rewilding

0	What's the size of the Glencrombie Estate?	*50,000 hectares*
1	According to the presenter, what activities attract visitors to the Scottish Highlands?	
2	What creatures inhabited the region in Roman times?	
3	What happened to the forests in the 18th century?	
4	How have the deer affected the landscape?	
5	According to Donald Christie, where have wolves been successfully reintroduced?	
6	Why does Fiona believe it will be impossible to reintroduce wolves?	
7	What does Fiona say needs to be protected?	
8	What other benefits does Donald believe the scheme would have?	

Four-word sentence completion

p7fp8s

5 You are going to listen to a podcast episode about a water purification system. First you will have 45 seconds to study the task below, then you will hear the recording twice. While listening, complete the sentences (1–8) using a maximum of four words. Write your answers in the spaces provided. The first one (0) has been done for you.

After the second listening, you will have 45 seconds to check your answers.

The drinkable book

0	The World Health Organisation says that the number of deaths from water-related illnesses is equal to the _____ .	*population of Los Angeles*
1	In many parts of the world, getting clean water can be time-consuming and _____ .	
2	The aim of the *Drinkable Book Project* is to make water purification _____ .	
3	The pages of the drinkable book can be used as _____ .	
4	The silver and copper nanoparticles on the paper _____ .	
5	To use the drinkable book, you first tear out a page and put it _____ .	
6	There's no need to worry about the silver nanoparticles because they are _____ .	
7	The WATERisLIFE charity is requesting donations towards _____ .	
8	So far, the sheets have been made with the help of _____ .	

Language in use

Tips and tricks

Banked gap-fill (BGF)

- While reading, think of a word that could fit the gap, then check the words in the bank. Which of them comes closest to what you had in mind?
- Remember to check the sentence before and after the gap to make sure your word fits.

Word formation (WF)

- First decide what kind of word (noun, verb, etc.) you need to complete the gap. Then change the given word to the correct form.
- Watch out in case a plural form, third-person singular -s, past tense or an opposite is required.
- There may be more than one correct answer.
- Check your spelling!

Multiple choice (MC)

- While reading, think of a word that could fit the gap, then check the four options. Which of them comes closest to what you had in mind?
- The options given might test your knowledge of grammar or vocabulary. Are you given four different forms of the same word or four different words as options? The option you choose should be correct in meaning and form.

Editing (ED)

- Read the instructions carefully because the number of correct lines can vary. The correct example line does not count.
- Look for short words like prepositions, conjunctions, modal verbs or adverbs.
- Reading a difficult line from right to left can help you focus more on individual words.
- The first and last word of a line are never wrong.
- A word that is in the line more than once is never wrong.

Open gap-fill (OGF)

- Every gap must be filled with exactly one word. Contractions such as *don't* or *I'm* are one word.
- If you can't think of a word right away, decide what kind of word (modal verb, linking word, article, etc.) you need to complete the gap. Then go through possible options in your head.
- There is often more than one correct answer.
- Watch out in case a plural form, past tense or third-person singular -s is required.
- Check your spelling!

You can find the answer key to all tasks online.
Go to www.oebv.at and type in this code: g55m3g.

Multiple choice

1 Read the text about online advertising. Some words are missing. Choose the correct answer (A, B, C or D) for each gap (1–15). Put a cross (☒) in the correct box. The first one (0) has been done for you.

Easy targets

Games, videos, news stories, social media posts and memes. Online advertisers often **(0)** ______ their marketing messages as entertainment or information. You may know the difference, **(1)** ______ children?

Online advertisers are using increasingly sophisticated marketing techniques, making it harder for young people to recognise when they are being **(2)** ______ to. Often, sponsored social media posts aren't labelled as advertising at all; **(3)** ______ , tagging, mentioning or thanking a brand can be considered sufficient. Many of the young people we work with are definitely not aware posts are sponsored. They genuinely believe the opinions are an honest reflection of the poster's views – why **(4)** ______ they be? When advertising is labelled, it is often so discreet that young people don't spot it. Less than a quarter of 8- to 11-year-olds and only one third of 12- to 15-year-olds can correctly identify sponsored links on Google **(5)** ______ they feature the word 'Ad' in a coloured box.

Marketers now make **(6)** ______ of social media to promote their brands because young consumers are more likely to look to YouTubers, bloggers and other influencers for purchasing advice. **(7)** ______ , one in three online users aged 12 to 15 are unaware that vloggers may be paid to endorse a product. Young people need to be informed about these discreet forms of advertising **(8)** ______ about techniques like tobacco companies' use of social media stars to target young people.

They may also spend more than they can afford. The number of younger people **(9)** ______ debt advice has been increasing in **(10)** ______ , with up to 8.3 million people in the UK unable to pay off debts or household bills. **(11)** ______ show that materialistic attitudes (wanting more and more material things) can affect well-being by creating a sense **(12)** ______ loneliness and damaging self-esteem or relationships.

Children are particularly **(13)** ______ to marketing messages. Personal devices (smartphones, tablets, smart and other gadgets) **(14)** ______ companies to reach youngsters directly, and more persuasively, **(15)** ______ . Branded websites, advergames, viral ads and social media marketing have blurred the lines between entertainment, information and advertising, making it difficult to recognise commercial content.

0	A are creating	☐	B are presenting	☐	C disguise	☒	D mask	☐
1	A but also	☐	B and may	☐	C but do	☐	D and can	☐
2	A directed	☐	B attracted	☐	C promised	☐	D sold	☐
3	A besides	☐	B instead	☐	C in addition	☐	D nevertheless	☐
4	A can	☐	B might	☐	C wouldn't	☐	D mustn't	☐
5	A also when	☐	B even though	☐	C but seldom	☐	D however rarely	☐
6	A experiences	☐	B benefit	☐	C advantage	☐	D use	☐
7	A Consequently	☐	B Thus	☐	C Yet	☐	D Admittedly	☐
8	A as well	☐	B as well as	☐	C concerning	☐	D concerned	☐
9	A searching	☐	B who have searched	☐	C seeking	☐	D that was seeking	☐
10	A the last time	☐	B recent years	☐	C a short interval	☐	D these days	☐
11	A Several researchers would	☐	B Other studies	☐	C Different researchers can	☐	D Various studies	☐
12	A for	☐	B about	☐	C of	☐	D in	☐
13	A susceptible	☐	B formed	☐	C guided	☐	D attractive	☐
14	A ensure	☐	B enable	☐	C have made	☐	D would allow	☐
15	A as ever before	☐	B than ever after	☐	C as ever after	☐	D than ever before	☐

Banked gap-fill

2 **Read the text about a celebrity animal. Some parts are missing. Choose the correct part (A–R) for each gap (1–15). There are two extra parts that you should not use. Write your answers in the boxes provided. The first one (0) has been done for you.**

Jumbo

The story of how a word got its meaning is often interesting. **(0)** ______ the word 'jumbo', which describes an enormous jet plane. **(1)** ______ this is the meaning we are probably most familiar with, the word is also widely used in advertising. For instance, we select a jumbo pack from the supermarket shelf **(2)** ______ of good value for money. But why 'jumbo'? The answer is a world-famous 19th-century zoo and circus elephant called Jumbo.

Jumbo was gigantic, even for an elephant, which is why his name **(3)** ______ be used to describe anything much larger than average. **(4)** ______ , he was around 4 metres tall. **(5)** ______ where the word 'jumbo' itself comes from is uncertain, but it **(6)** ______ be most probably of African origin.

(7) ______ , Jumbo spent almost his entire life with humans. His mother having been killed by hunters in his native Sudan, he was captured, sold, and transported across sea and land, eventually ending up in a Parisian zoo. **(8)** ______ how stressful this must have been for a young wild animal. He was **(9)** ______ of the mother who, in his natural habitat, he **(10)** ______ have left for many more years to come.

It was during his time at London Zoo, to which he was later transferred, that Jumbo started to gain fame. No trip to the zoo was complete without a ride on Jumbo, and he was a great favourite, **(11)** ______ . However, in 1882 London Zoo made the **(12)** ______ decision to sell Jumbo. They feared that, as an adult male, he may become too dangerously **(13)** ______ and therefore a problem to handle. In response to the public protests that followed, the zoo tried to reverse the business deal, **(14)** ______ , and Jumbo crossed the Atlantic to join an American circus.

(15) ______ his reputation had gone before him, Jumbo was also hugely successful in America, participating in many events, such as the opening of the Brooklyn Bridge. His life came to a tragic end one night in 1885, when he was hit and killed by a train at a railway station. But Jumbo's name lives on.

A	Although	G	Exactly	M	Needless to say
B	Astonishingly	H	hardly ever respectful	N	Since
C	but in vain	I	hardly surprisingly	~~O~~	Take
D	came to	J	Imagine	P	taking care
E	controversial	K	in expectation	Q	unpredictable
F	deprived	L	is thought to	R	would not

0	1	2	3	4	5	6	7	8	9	10	11	12	13	14	15
O															

Open gap-fill

3 Read the text about how a couple got to know each other. Some words are missing. Complete the text by writing <u>one</u> word for each gap (1–15) in the spaces provided. The first one (0) has been done for you.

Biscuits

This is the story of how I met Anne. It sounds like the kind of boy-meets-girl story you'd be more (0) ______ to come across in a film than in real life, but it's true.

It all started with Gem. Gem is my retriever, and it was (1) ______ to his love of biscuits that I made Anne's acquaintance. My mother, (2) ______ main aim in life is to spoil Gem whenever she can, always shares her biscuit with him. Annoyingly, she does it in (3) ______ of my protests that it's bad for him. Anyway, this means that Gem associates the female gender with delicious things to eat.

So, one day, I was playing with Gem in the park when a girl came along, sat down on a bench and (4) ______ out her packed lunch. She obviously wanted to take (5) ______ of the fine, sunny weather in her lunch break. Everything went well (6) ______ a while: the girl ate her sandwiches and Gem chased his ball. And then the girl unwrapped a biscuit. In an instant, Gem was racing in the (7) ______ of the bench, barking joyfully, certain of a treat. But (8) ______ of breaking off a bit of biscuit for him, she shrieked, jumped up and treated him in a very unfriendly way. Running over to pull Gem away, I was (9) ______ very abruptly that I was not fit to keep a dog if I (10) ______ it to attack people. Well, how could she know that Gem wouldn't hurt a fly? I must admit, however, that he can get a bit over-excited when it (11) ______ to a biscuit. I apologised and eventually the girl calmed down and we got chatting. (12) ______ the time she had to go back to work, Gem had been forgiven for his bad (13) ______ and we were all friends.

The girl was Anne, of course, and we've been together (14) ______ two years now. Between you and me, I think Anne is now the one that sometimes feeds Gem biscuits, (15) ______ she always denies it. But I suppose he has deserved a treat for bringing us together.

0	likely	8	
1		9	
2		10	
3		11	
4		12	
5		13	
6		14	
7		15	

Word formation

4 Read the text about examinations. Some words are missing. Change the word in brackets to form the missing word for each gap (1–15). Write your answers in the spaces provided. The first one (0) has been done for you.

Put to the test

Written exams have their critics. Some believe that exams test only short-term memory and claim that, although passing an exam will get the candidates a qualification, they will forget much of what they studied soon afterwards. Others believe that exams are not an (0) ______ (effect) way of testing for those who suffer from nerves because, when they are under (1) ______ (press), their performance may not reflect their true ability.

Exams (2) ______ (doubt) have their drawbacks. However, they are perhaps the most (3) ______ (rely) way of establishing what an individual is capable of at a given moment. Besides, an exam is a test of many things other than simply how well the candidate can (4) ______ (memory) facts and figures – which is not to say that this in itself is a (5) ______ (point) aim. Possessing a certain amount of general and specialist knowledge is still the (6) ______ (found) for success in the professional world. In any case, a worthwhile exam will ensure that what is tested is not simply the (7) ______ (repeat) of knowledge but the skill of applying that knowledge in new situations.

The whole (8) ______ (proceed) of taking an important exam requires qualities of character that are essential in everyday professional and academic life. One has to commit to a goal and prepare (9) ______ (one) appropriately, which means working consistently and with (10) ______ (determined). During the actual exam, stamina is required to be able to write at (11) ______ (long) in a relatively short period of time. And one must be able to overcome those absolutely (12) ______ (understand) feelings of anxiety in order to focus on the task at hand.

On opening the exam paper, there can be a moment of panic when everything seems terrifyingly unfamiliar. However, there comes that moment of (13) ______ (relieve), when the words start to flow or the figures start to fall into place, (14) ______ (provide) that one is well prepared, of course. For some confident candidates, it is even a case of the (15) ______ (trick) the question, the greater the sense of satisfaction gained from tackling it. But one thing is certain: all candidates are happy when the exam is over.

0	effective	8	
1		9	
2		10	
3		11	
4		12	
5		13	
6		14	
7		15	

Editing

5 **Read the text about the origins of a famous book. In most lines (1–15) there is a word that should not be there. Write these words in the spaces provided. 2–4 lines are correct. Make a ✓ in the space if the line is correct. There are two examples (0, 00) at the beginning.**

Robinson Crusoe

Text	Answer	Line
Robinson Crusoe is regarded by many as the first English novel. When	✓	(0)
it has appeared in the year 1719, it was in every respect a great success.	has	(00)
Although a few people nowadays have read the book all the way through,	______	(1)
everyone has heard of the shipwrecked sailor who manages it to survive on a	______	(2)
remote island. Written by Daniel Defoe, it is supposed to have been inspired	______	(3)
by then the true story of Alexander Selkirk. Selkirk was a sailor who argued	______	(4)
with the captain of the ship what he was sailing on about whether it was safe.	______	(5)
He then chose to leave the ship and stay behind on an island rather than risk	______	(6)
drowning. As it turned unfortunately out, Selkirk had been right because the	______	(7)
ship later sank. It is known that Defoe and Selkirk met instead, so it is more	______	(8)
than likely that the novel is indeed based on Selkirk's experience. However,	______	(9)
Selkirk was being rescued after just over four years on his island, while	______	(10)
Robinson Crusoe, the fictional character, is cut off hardly from civilisation for	______	(11)
28 years. And since there are several other differences between Selkirk's	______	(12)
story and that about Crusoe. Despite of the fact that Defoe obviously used his	______	(13)
imagination as well as the real-life adventure of Selkirk, Selkirk's adventure	______	(14)
is general acknowledged as being the main source of inspiration. In 1966	______	(15)
the island Selkirk inhabited was renamed Robinson Crusoe Island.		

Writing

The information and tasks provided in the following sections will help you improve your texts, which will be graded according to the assessment criteria generally used in Austria. These criteria are task achievement, organisation and layout, lexical and structural range, lexical and structural accuracy.

The exercises below will focus on the most common challenges that might occur in text production. For more information on the B2 Assessment Scale and on task type conventions, please refer to the *SRDP* (*standardisierte Reife- und Diplomprüfung*) website.

You can find the answer key to all tasks online. Go to www.oebv.at and type in this code: g55m3g.

Improving lexical and structural range

Use strong, expressive adjectives and adverbs

1 **Try to avoid using *very*. Match adjectives 1–12 to the expressions with a similar meaning (a–l).**

1 ancient
2 basic
3 deafening
4 distraught
5 enthusiastic
6 exhausted
7 furious
8 intriguing
9 spotless
10 terrified
11 thrilling
12 vital

a very important
b very afraid
c very angry
d very interested
e very interesting
f very old
g very clean
h very upset
i very exciting
j very simple
k very loud
l very tired

2 **Complete the table below by filling in the more 'basic' version of the adjectives.**

(very) bad ▪ (very) beautiful ▪ (very) cold ▪ (very) funny ▪ (very) good ▪ (very) hot ▪ (very) hungry ▪ (very) sad ▪ (very) ugly ▪ (very) worried

1 fantastic, fabulous, excellent, superb			
2 awful, horrible, terrible, repellent			
3 devastated		7 hideous	
4 hilarious		8 freezing	
5 distressed		9 scorching	
6 gorgeous		10 starving	

3 **Use adverbs of degree to sound more natural. Match the expressions from the box to their German equivalents.**

a bit (*infml.*) ▪ a little ▪ absolutely ▪ completely ▪ deeply ▪ extremely ▪ fairly ▪ pretty (*infml.*) ▪ quite ▪ rather ▪ really ▪ slightly ▪ somewhat ▪ totally (*infml.*) ▪ utterly

1 *ein bisschen* ____________________

2 *ziemlich* ____________________

3 *sehr* ____________________

4 **Use sentence adverbs to emphasise your opinion when appropriate. Find the most fitting alternative for the sentence adverbs below. Sometimes there is more than one correct answer.**

Clearly ▪ Evidently ▪ Fortunately ▪ Funnily ▪ Honestly ▪ Sadly ▪ Surprisingly

1 Unfortunately/ ____________________, some of your promises were not fulfilled.

2 Luckily/ ____________________, nobody realised what I had been doing.

3 Frankly/ ____________________, I wouldn't dare to question this.

4 Obviously/ ____________________, a solution has to be found.

5 Strangely/ ____________________, not a single listener applauded.

6 Apparently/ ____________________, they are planning a new power plant.

7 Unexpectedly/ ____________________, the weather changed again.

5 **Study the sentence adverbs in the box and decide which ones can be used to start the sentences.**

a Actually b Admittedly c Basically d Hopefully e Ideally f Surprisingly g Undoubtedly

1 a, b, f ____________________, our neighbour didn't seem to mind the noise.

2 ____________________, I'll be able to join you there.

3 ____________________, you should have informed us about your change of plans much earlier.

4 ____________________, none of the candidates chose topic 3.

5 ____________________, the consequences of this step had not been considered.

6 ____________________, most people say they would prefer to live in the city.

7 ____________________, I haven't tried to improve my performance.

Use a variety of expressions and structures to show your vocabulary range and avoid repetition or prompt lifting.[1]

6 **Find the missing synonyms.**

1 significant, essential, central, crucial — important
2 demanding, challenging, problematic, tough — d________
3 a benefit/plus/pro — an a________
4 a drawback/minus/weakness — a d________
5 high-priced, costly, pricey — e________
6 to despise/dislike/detest — to h________
7 to adore/admire/fancy/care for/appreciate — to l________
8 an opinion, a view/thought/belief — an i________
9 to present/indicate/demonstrate — to s________

7 **Decide which of the sentences (a or b) is more formal. Highlight the expressions and structures that make them more formal.**

	a	b
1	I reckon it's going to be difficult to set up rules like that.	Apparently, such rules will be difficult to establish.
2	Not until the 1990s did the internet play such a vital role.	The internet wasn't really important before the 1990s.
3	It's news to me that such measures were going to be introduced.	I was completely unaware that such measures were to be implemented.
4	The purpose of this report is to discuss a survey on teenagers' leisure activities.	In this report, I want to discuss a survey on what teenagers do in their free time.
5	Evidently, there are no resources available to establish protected areas for these endangered species.	It is obvious that we won't be able to set up protected areas for these endangered animals.
6	We've got to deal with this matter soon.	This matter needs to be dealt with urgently.
7	A similar phenomenon can be discovered when it comes to e-readers.	You will find the same situation when you look at e-readers.
8	Additionally, I would strongly recommend that young people read plays by Shakespeare.	I think young people should also read plays by Shakespeare.
9	People often say that they are not influenced by ads.	More often than not, people claim not to be influenced by advertisements.
10	This opportunity would allow me to prove my qualifications.	If you give me the chance, I can show you that I'm qualified.
11	I would like to apologise for not replying earlier.	I'm sorry it's taken me so long to answer your email.
12	This country produces a lot of food, but ordinary people haven't got much to eat.	Despite the fact that more than enough food is produced within the country, ordinary people have little to eat.

[1] **prompt lifting:** copying expressions/chunks of language from the prompt

8 **There is a wide variety of structures that can convey the same meaning. Read the five options and cross out the one which is wrong.**

1 a Another aspect worth considering when talking about …
b Another aspect that should be considered when talking about …
c Another aspect one ought to consider when talking about …
d Another aspect considering when talking about …
e Another aspect to consider when talking about …

2 a Young people are not the only ones who profit from such summer jobs.
b Young people are not the only ones to profit from such summer jobs.
c Young people are not the only ones to be profited from such summer jobs.
d Young people are not the only ones profiting from such summer jobs.
e Young people are not the only ones who will profit from such summer jobs.

3 a Local shops which offer such a service clearly benefit from this situation.
b Local shops offering such a service clearly benefit from this situation.
c If local shops offer such a service, they will clearly benefit from this situation.
d Local shops capable of offering such a service will clearly benefit from this situation.
e Local shops able to offering such a service clearly benefit from this situation.

4 a When I realised that your company provides such a bad service, I was deeply disappointed.
b On realising that your company provides such a bad service, I was deeply disappointed.
c When I realised that such a bad service is provided by your company, I was deeply disappointed.
d When your company had been realised to provide only such a bad service, I was deeply disappointed.
e I was deeply disappointed when I realised that your company provides such a bad service.

5 a Roughly a fifth of the interviewees claimed that they never watched films showing such scenes.
b Roughly a fifth of the interviewees claimed never to watch films showing such scenes.
c Roughly a fifth of the interviewees claimed that they never watched films to show such scenes.
d Roughly a fifth of the people who were interviewed claimed that they never watched films showing such scenes.
e Roughly a fifth of the interviewees claimed that they never watched films that showed such scenes.

9 **Put the chunks into the correct order to create meaningful sentences.**

1 that give us energy / can be found in meat and fish / and keep us healthy / a high number of proteins
2 caused by cars / the main reason is / by the amount of pollution / that our environment is seriously endangered
3 a large majority stated / about the future / of the 400 students younger than 20 / they were basically optimistic
4 if you could inform us / it would be really helpful / on things like public transport / about special discounts
5 stress is on the rise in our modern world / on people for various reasons / it is generally believed that / as more and more demands are made
6 as I gained valuable insight / when providing activities for small children / into challenges that arise / this has been a great experience

Improving accuracy

Spelling

1 **Study the expressions below. One of them is correct, the other one is misspelled. Circle the correct ones.**

	a	b		a	b
1	to accommodate	to accomodate	21	immidiate	immediate
2	to acomplish	to accomplish	22	length	lenght
3	address	adress	23	lovely	lovly
4	advertisement	advertisment	24	necessary	neccessery
5	to affect	to effect	25	noticeable	noticable
6	awfull	awful	26	permanant	permanent
7	babies	babys	27	pleasant	pleasent
8	business	buisness	28	to possess	to posses
9	coming	comming	29	to practize	to practise
10	committee	commitee	30	preference	preferance
11	costumer	customer	31	to recieve	to receive
12	definitly	definitely	32	to recommend	to recomend
13	developement	development	33	safty	safety
14	dissapoint	disappoint	34	seperate	separate
15	diffrent	different	35	stopping	stoping
16	to embarrass	to embarass	36	succeed	suceed
17	finally	finaly	37	tipps	tips
18	foreward	forward	38	tried	tryed
19	fourty	forty	39	untill	until
20	heared	heard	40	widely	widly

2 **Explain the difference between the words below. Can you think of more tricky words?**

1 quit – quiet – quite
2 weather – whether
3 advice – advise
4 prove – proof
5 loose – lose
6 accept – except

3 **Each line of the text below contains a spelling mistake. Cross the misspelled word out and write the correct version on the line provided.**

Director Tom Hooper manages to show George VI's issues realy well. really (1)
All the actors and actresses are well choosen and deliver an exceptional ______ (2)
performance, especially Colin Firth, by whom I was pleasently surprised. ______ (3)
He plays the part of the stammerer brilliantly and extremly convincingly. ______ (4)
Therefor, he absolutely deserved to get an Academy Award for this ______ (5)
impressive performance. All in all, I really recommend *The King's Speach* ______ (6)
– it's a must-see!

Punctuation

4 **Read the sentences below and correct them. The commas are either not necessary or missing.**

1 However it is quite difficult to do the task on one's own.
2 You can always take a rest, if you feel frustrated.
3 As I see it the Austrian education system is definitely superior to the American system.
4 Then I realised, that nothing would work out as I had imagined.
5 I couldn't find time for anything else, such as shopping for example.
6 Maybe the best thing you can do is, to take a break after school.
7 In fact you cannot really trust film classifications which makes them virtually meaningless.
8 When I was younger I used to eat sweets more often.
9 I have already worked as an assistant at Vandalia High where I gained valuable experience.
10 Another essential element of great schools is of course excellent teachers.
11 Most of the interviewees watch TV for about three hours a day which takes up more than half their free time.
12 Actually I hate punctuation rules, because they are so tricky.

5 **Insert the six commas that are missing in this paragraph.**

Thirdly the question remains how we can manage to rise above our prejudices. As the development of prejudices is a vital human strategy to deal with the unknown I think we cannot ever be completely rid of them. What can be done however is to re-evaluate these prejudices by interacting with other people. The more interaction we have the more experiences we can gather in order to prove or disprove our own hypotheses of different things. In turn this enables us to revise the pictures in our minds to be able to cope better with similar situations the next time.

6 **Rewrite the text below to include capital letters and necessary punctuation.**

bath is a medium sized city in somerset england it has roughly 86000 inhabitants and goes back to a roman foundation from the first century the site of the famous ancient bathing complex now houses a world class museum which offers a fascinating insight into life in the city 2000 years ago an estimated 625 million people visited the area in 2018 the visitors interest also focused on the famous pump rooms our childrens programme has definitely contributed to this success said the mayor of bath

Working on text-type-specific challenges

Titles in essays, articles and blog posts

Titles in essays	Titles in articles and blog posts
They should be factual, precise and make clear what the essay will discuss. Ideally, they foreshadow the writer's opinion.	They should be catchy, bold or provocative so as to get the readers' attention. They can address the readers directly.

1 **The titles below all refer to a writing task on books and their film adaptations. Decide which one(s) would be more suitable for an article (A), which one(s) for an essay (E) and which one(s) should be dropped (D) as they make no sense for either text type.**

	A	E	D
1 Book or film, that is the question	☐	☐	☐
2 Let your imagination run free!	☐	☐	☐
3 Books have many advantages	☐	☐	☐
4 Why books are better than films	☐	☐	☐
5 Books	☐	☐	☐
6 Films: The better books?	☐	☐	☐

2 **The titles below all refer to a writing task promoting the idea of staying at home for one's holiday. Decide which one(s) is/are great for an article or blog post (A/B) and which one(s) would be more suitable for an essay on this topic (E).**

	A/B	E
1 Don't go away! Stay!	☐	☐
2 The advantages of staying at home in the summer	☐	☐
3 East or West? Home is Best!	☐	☐
4 Ever tried a staycation?	☐	☐
5 Why staying at home for one's holiday is a good choice	☐	☐
6 People should stay at home for their holiday	☐	☐

3 **Match the following titles to the topics of the blog posts. There is one title you won't need.**

1 travel	a Try bouldering!
2 fashion	b Why vote?
3 food	c Save the bears!
4 art	d Forget about calories. Try this!
5 sport	e Beat is back
6 music	f It doesn't have to be Picasso
7 health	g Why not New Zealand this year?
8 politics	h Sugar can kill you!
	i It's a must-have this spring

Language and organisation in reports

4 **Match the phrases on the right to the percentages on the left. Draw lines.**

88%	nearly a third
80%	around 90 percent
72%	roughly a quarter
69%	approximately a fifth
48%	exactly eight in ten
43%	almost half
32%	less than three quarters
27%	more than two thirds
19%	just about one in ten
11%	a little over 40 percent
8%	slightly under ten percent
5%	merely five percent

5 **Read part of a prompt asking for a report on teenage alcohol consumption and decide on the most suitable subject line and headings.**

The British government is trying to reduce alcohol consumption among teenagers and needs to gather information on this. Therefore, 200 young people were interviewed on when they started drinking and where they usually drink alcohol.

Choose the most suitable subject line:

1 Alcohol
2 Drinking habits of teenagers
3 Why teenagers drink
4 Teenagers drink a lot of alcohol

Choose the most suitable heading for this content point:

- explain why teenagers choose certain locations

1 Reasons
2 Favourite places
3 Reasons for choosing particular locations
4 Explanations for teenagers

Choose the most suitable heading for this content point:

- suggest how to prevent teenagers from drinking alcohol

1 Suggestions for teenagers
2 Recommendations
3 Recommendations to improve the situation
4 How can the government prevent teenagers from drinking alcohol?

Language in formal emails

6 **Match the phrases to use in formal emails (1–6) to the parts of an email (a–f).**

a giving reasons for writing
b stating a complaint
c introducing a request
d applying for a position
e asking for information
f ending the email

1 ☐

Could you possibly give me some information on …?
First of all, I would like to know …
My final question is …
If possible, I also need to know …
I (also) have a question about …

2 ☐

I am writing to express my dissatisfaction about …
I am afraid I have to draw your attention to …
Unfortunately, … was not really what I expected.
I am afraid I was not (completely/fully) satisfied with …
I find it disappointing that …
You do not seem to realise that …
I am quite surprised that an organisation like yours …

3 ☐

I think I am well suited to …
My personal experience of … started when …
I am experienced in …
In addition to my academic studies, …
When I was working at …, …
Whilst doing volunteer work at …, I became highly competent in …
Although I have no previous experience in …, …
My strengths are …

4 ☐

I am writing with reference to …
I am writing to you in connection with/with regard to/concerning …
I am writing to complain about …
I am writing to ask for further/additional information on/regarding …
I am writing in response to …
I would like to express my interest in …
I would like to apply for the post/position of …
I am writing (in order) to inquire/confirm/inform you …
As promised/As we discussed, I am writing to send you …

5 ☐

I am very interested in …
Would you mind sending me …?
I was wondering if you could/whether it would be possible (for you) …
I would be grateful if you could …
I would really appreciate some help with …
Would you be so kind as to …?

6 ☐

(In the meantime,) If you need more information, …
I am looking forward to hearing from you.
If you require any further information about …,
If you have any more questions about …, feel free to contact me …
I would welcome the opportunity to discuss further details …
Please, do not hesitate to get in touch …
I hope this answers all your questions …

7 **Match the informal expressions (1–14) to their more formal equivalents (a–n).**

1 to need	6 to call	11 good for
2 boss	7 to want	12 to help
3 whole	8 happy	13 a lot of
4 sad	9 to get	14 job
5 to call off	10 okay	

a would like	f position	k disappointing/-ed
b to assist	g entire	l to contact
c beneficial	h to cancel	m pleased
d to receive	i numerous	n acceptable
e superior	j to require	

Working on articles

1 **Match the parts of the article (1–4) to the text type requirements they need to meet (a–d).**

1 title
2 introduction
3 body paragraphs
4 conclusion

a Give your readership something to think about. Give them the feeling that they have not wasted their time reading it.
b Give the readers an idea of what the article is going to be about. It should be catchy, bold or provocative.
c Arouse the readers' interest and make them want to continue reading.
d Develop the content points (bullet points). Smooth transitions between the paragraphs will make reading the article enjoyable.

2 **Study the prompt below. It contains all the information you need. Identify:**

1 text type ______
2 readership ______
3 topic ______
4 details of the topic ______
5 required number of words (+/– 10%) ______

An international youth magazine has started a series of articles on summer jobs for young people. As it is promising €500 to the writers of the best article, you have decided to send one in.

In your article you should:

- point out the importance of a summer job for young people's future
- explain how companies can benefit from employing young people
- recommend a summer job that young people might like

Give your article a title. Write around 250 words.

3 **Brainstorm ideas and cluster them, take notes or draw mindmaps. For example:**

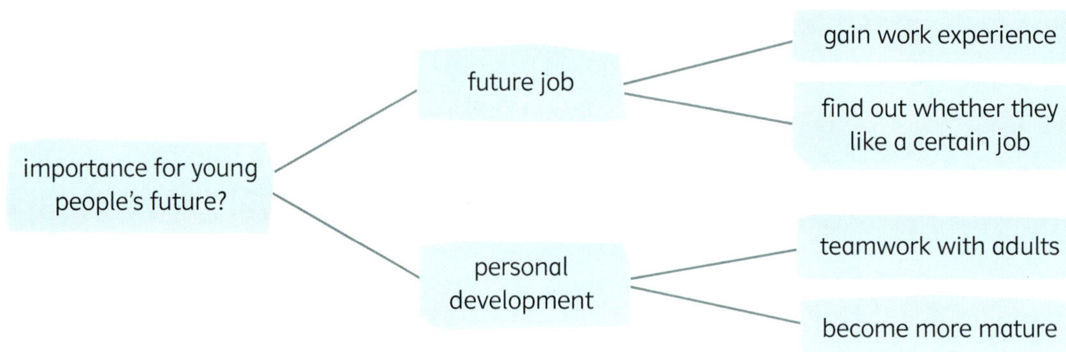

4 **Read the writing task on summer jobs again, then go through the titles below. Most of them are catchy, bold or provocative. Identify the ones that are not ideal.**[2]

1 Ready to work?
2 Summer jobs – summer flops
3 Go and get the job!
4 The advantages of taking on a summer job
5 It's not just about the cash
6 A summer job – an opportunity not to be missed
7 Why young people should have a summer job

5 **Read the different introductions for the article and decide which of them are well written. The questions below will help you with your decision.**

1 Is the reader addressed?
2 Is the language used lively and expressive?
3 Can you find examples of repetition that are used on purpose to attract the reader's attention?

a Many teenagers spend their summer break working because, as most people know, if they don't work in the summer, they will probably be broke for the rest of the year. Yet, there are many other reasons – apart from the money – for working during your summer holidays.

b Have you ever wondered why you should work during your summer holidays? Have you ever asked yourself why on earth you should spend your well-deserved free time in an office instead of relaxing on a beach? Well, summer jobs are actually more beneficial than you might think.

c Every teenager knows them. Every teenager hates them. Right, I'm talking about summer jobs. Of course, they are not everyone's favourite way of spending the summer holidays. But wouldn't you agree that with some work experience, your future could look much brighter?

d Admit it! You sometimes get bored during your endless summer holidays. This is the perfect solution: Look for a job, earn some money and profit from the experiences you will have.

e More and more young people decide to spend their summer holidays, at least partially, earning their own money and improving their skills with a summer job. The following article is going to outline why young people should definitely take this opportunity and find a job that suits them.

[2] See p. 36 for more work on titles for articles.

6 **Look at the topic sentences below and decide which content point (bullet point) they introduce.**

a Finally, I would like to share my experience of a perfect summer job with you.
b Actually, it's not only students who will profit from doing a summer job but also the companies involved.
c Young people especially like summer jobs where they can help and see positive results of their effort.
d Great news! Not only you but also your employer will profit from your work.
e So, are you now thinking about a suitable job for yourself?
f No doubt about it, summer jobs for students are definitely useful for a variety of reasons.
g What's more, summer jobs are not only beneficial to young people.

7 a **Put the sentences below in the correct order to build a meaningful paragraph that addresses content point 1.**

a Additionally, a summer job provides the chance to find out where your strengths and passions lie, and maybe you can already build connections with future employers.
b Earning money is just one of the many advantages of a summer job.
c Besides, what's bad about getting to know new people or even finding friends?
d To start with, you will be able to have experiences no one can take away from you, and you will acquire new skills that might come in handy later in life.

b **Put the sentences below in the correct order to build a meaningful paragraph that addresses content point 2.**

a Young people have so many great ideas that could be assets for their employers.
b Finally, companies might find someone who they could hire permanently.
c Not only young people profit from working during the summer but also the companies that employ them.
d As you can see, summer jobs are a plus for both job seekers and work providers.
e What's more, it's useful to have an extra person in the company, especially at times when so many employees are on holiday.

8 **Decide which of the conclusions below give the readers something to think about and move them to take action.**

1 Whatever you decide to do, whether you have good or bad experiences, it will be worth it as you'll at least have an entertaining story to tell. So get started and write your application.

2 So, if you fancy all the new experiences, benefits and fun, then join the growing number of summer jobbers. You won't regret your decision to improve your skills whilst enjoying new things.

3 Summing up, summer jobs are not only important for young people but also for the businesses that offer them. The main thing is to find a job that you like doing.

Working on essays

1 **Match the parts of the essay (1–4) to the text type requirements they need to meet (a–d).**

1 title
2 introduction
3 body paragraphs
4 conclusion

a Briefly present the arguments you intend to develop in the main body.
b Introduce each content point (bullet point) with a topic sentence. Develop the content points dealing with one argument per body paragraph. Support your arguments with examples/evidence and reason(s).
c Be factual and precise and make clear what the essay will discuss.
d Summarise your opinion based on the arguments given in the body paragraphs.

2 **Study the task below and answer the questions.**

1 Who is going to read the essay?
2 What question do you need to answer?
3 Which three of the following stylistic features should be avoided in an essay: contractions, passive structures, personal pronouns, conditionals, direct questions.

An international health forum is concerned about people's sugar intake. It wants to know what teenagers think about measures that might keep people from eating too many sugary products. They are asking for essays. You have decided to send one in.

In your essay you should discuss if:

- higher taxes on sugary products might help
- advertisements for sugary products should be banned
- schools can help raise people's awareness

Give your essay a title. Write around 400 words.

3 **Look at the eight titles below and tick the four that are factual, precise and make clear what the essay will discuss.**[3]

1 How to reduce people's sugar intake
2 Appropriate initiatives to reduce the consumption of sugary products
3 Take action against the consumption of sugary products!
4 Why measures against excessive sugar intake will not help
5 Taxes on sugary products
6 Sugar, we are going down
7 People are eating too many sugary products
8 Measures against sugar intake are necessary to improve people's health

4 **Read the introductions (1–4) and match them to the feedback below (a–d).**

1 For decades, the average sugar intake per person has been increasing, as has the number of overweight people. A variety of ways to fight this common health problem of our privileged society have been discussed, but none of them has worked so far. So it is time to stop talking and take action. In order to successfully reduce the consumption of sugar in our country, specific regulations for sweets are needed. ☐

2 Obesity has been proven to be a major health problem of our time among all age groups, with high-sugar products being one of the main elements of an unhealthy lifestyle. Programmes are being considered to address this problem adequately. However, many of these ideas, such as introducing higher taxes, banning advertisements on sugary products and starting educational programmes at school, are ineffective. They restrict freedom of choice, and this reduces personal liberty. ☐

3 It's a fact that sugar is known to be bad for people's health. The problem is that in most cases this knowledge does not keep them from consuming it. So we need to ask ourselves: What can be done to stop people from consuming so much sugar? How may higher taxes and a ban on sugary products help, and how can schools raise awareness? ☐

4 Sugar has become a main ingredient in food around the world. Many people consume it on a daily basis and, most of the time, they do it without realising what they are eating. Many people cannot live without sugar, and for this reason, they consume too much every day. Unfortunately, this affects their health in a negative way. Also, it is a problem that most teenagers would rather buy fast food than cook healthy meals. The question is whether it would be helpful to introduce higher taxes on sugary products. ☐

a Clear thesis statement, but misleading information in the first sentence. Obesity as a health problem is not an issue in this essay.
b Thesis statement is inadequate. Lots of barely relevant information. The reader is not informed about the writer's opinion with regard to the measures as suggested in the content points. The last sentence indicates that the essay will only focus on the first content point. Apart from that, more complex structures could be used, and repetition should be avoided.
c Clear thesis statement, but the nature of the measures ("specific regulations") to be taken is vague and should ideally be specified.
d Thesis statement is missing. The reader is not informed about the writer's opinion with regard to the measures as suggested in the content points. Apart from that, direct questions should not be used.

5 **Read the four introductions again. Which one clearly indicates an essay in favour of measures against too much sugar consumption, which one an essay against measures to reduce sugar consumption?**

[3] See p. 36 for more work on titles for essays.

6 **Put the sentences below in the right order to create a coherent paragraph. Identify the topic sentence. Then decide which example deals with which content point.**

Example 1

a Whenever people use media, be it the internet, television or print, they are constantly exposed to advertisements. ☐

b What is more, advertisements for healthy snacks could subconsciously trick people into consuming healthier food. ☐

c Banning sweet advertisements would be an effective long-term solution to reduce people's sugar intake. [1]

d Therefore, fewer advertisements for sugary products will most likely decrease the number of these goods being purchased. ☐

e Many of these feature sugary products and, naturally, the more of them consumers see, the higher the chance that they will buy them. ☐

Example 2

a It makes good sense to encourage them early on to live a healthy lifestyle and educate them about its advantages. ☐

b Alternatively, a more successful idea may be to raise awareness of healthy habits in school-age children. ☐

c It would be most effective to give them some practical experience, for example in cooking workshops where young people learn to prepare healthy meals they can enjoy. ☐

d Of course, it is not sufficient to simply tell them to stop eating sweets. ☐

Example 3

a Consumers will look for the cheapest options available, thereby purchasing low-quality products, which will almost certainly be unhealthy. ☐

b It could be argued that increasing taxes on sugary products will encourage fewer customers to buy them, but, in fact, the opposite will be the case. ☐

c This way higher taxes on sweets would not be necessary. ☐

d To ensure people's health, prices for nutritious products such as vegetables and fruits should be lowered to make them more appealing. ☐

7 **Decide which of the two conclusions below is the better one. Give reasons.**

a In conclusion, it cannot be denied that sugary products pose a severe risk to our society's health. However, solutions can be found. Higher taxation on sweets, restrictions on advertising for certain products and health-oriented education at school all present effective ways to reduce the average sugar intake per person.

b Summing up, sugar consumption is a major issue in our society. It may trigger overweight, high blood pressure and other illnesses. However, the problem could be solved if governments raised taxes on all foods containing sugar.

Working on blogs

1 **Decide which are parts of a blog post and which are parts of a blog comment. Which are parts of both? Draw lines.**

Blog post

User name
Email address

Title

Introduction (1): Briefly refer to the blog post or blog comment. Make sure you fully understand it before you comment on it.

Introduction (2): Let the reader know what you are going to write about.

Main body: Develop the content points (bullet points), highlighting the personal significance of ideas and events.

Conclusion: Invite comments, give the reader something to think about or encourage him/her to take action.

Blog comment

2 **Rephrase the following expressions from the task below to avoid prompt lifting.**

1 you have found ______________________
2 is constantly increasing ______________________
3 ignore ______________________
4 especially annoying ______________________
5 make sense ______________________
6 act considerately ______________________

On a website for new blogs, you have found this one on rules and regulations:

daily_traveller
13 March, 5:47 p.m.

Just too many don'ts

... The number of signs telling us what to do and what not to do is constantly increasing. I'm afraid people will simply ignore them. Or, even worse, too many of them might even cause the opposite.

You have decided to comment on this blog post. In your blog comment you should:

- inform your readers about a sign you find especially annoying
- present a situation in which this sign makes sense
- suggest how to make people act considerately without it

Write around 250 words.

3 **Read the introductions for the blog comment and decide which of them does not clearly refer to the blog post above.**

1 Don't eat on the bus! Don't smoke at the train station! All these signs limit our freedom. I so agree with you that they're maddening.

2 I've just stumbled across your blog post and I can totally see your point. I also think that most people disregard signs or do things they shouldn't do because they think it's fun to break the rules.

3 I'd like to write about a sign that bothers me the most. It's the one that says "Don't step on the lawn". Think of a lawn in a park, for example. Aren't people meant to relax there?

4 Having read your blog post on rules and regulations, I can only say that I couldn't agree with you more. We're constantly surrounded by walls plastered in signs telling us what to do – it's really frustrating.

5 I've come across your blog post recently and I can only agree with what you are saying because I think that there are a lot of rules and regulations that are simply irritating. Wherever we are, signs tell us what we should or shouldn't do.

4 **Read the beginning of the blog comment below. Then read the ideas suggested for content point 2 and find evidence and reasons to support each of them.**

I've just read your blog post and I can absolutely relate to what you're saying. I agree that so many people no longer pay attention to signs or – even worse – do things they shouldn't because they think it's funny to break the rules.

A sign that is particularly irritating for me is the one that says "No dogs allowed here". This sign can be found in many places where it is obvious that you wouldn't bring a dog, for example, in a hospital. So why put it there? Isn't it evident that dog owners are responsible enough to think of that themselves? Especially in a hospital, there are so many things to consider, so many other important signs to be read, that the one saying "No dogs" is utterly superfluous.

Content point 2: *present a situation in which this sign makes sense*

Possible situation	**Evidence/Reasons**
1 children's playground	______________________
	______________________
2 cycle path	______________________
	______________________
3 spa	______________________
	______________________

Working on emails

1 **Match the parts of the email (1–4) to the text type requirements they need to meet (a–d).**

1 subject line
2 introduction
3 body paragraphs
4 conclusion

a Develop the content points (bullet points), highlighting the personal significance of ideas and events at the beginning of each paragraph.
b Let the recipient know what action you expect: stay in contact, give a refund, provide information, …
c Be clear, precise and accurate about what the email is about.
d State your reason for writing.

Layout:

From:
To:
Subject line:
Salutation
Introduction
Content point
Content point
Content point
Conclusion
Signing off

2 **Study the task below. Identify the recipient and the purpose of writing.**

You have found this advertisement in *Young Films*, an English magazine:

You have decided to send an email to Mr Sprite. In your email you should:

- explain why you would like the job
- outline your qualifications
- specify what you need to know about the job

Write around 250 words.

3 **Decide which two subject lines work best and which one does not make sense for the recipient.**

1 Actors wanted
2 Application for taking part in crowd scenes
3 Teendrama Productions
4 Harrison application for crowd scenes Innsbruck

4 **Choose the best introduction:**

Dear Mr Sprite,

1 I am writing to inquire about the position of actor in the crowd scenes of your new drama series.
2 I would like to take part in the crowd scenes of your new drama series, which you advertised in *Young Films*.
3 I am writing to express my interest in taking part in the film.

5 **Choose the better way to deal with content point 1:**

a My name is Gerald Harrer. I am 17 years old and I attend XY Gymnasium in Salzburg. I would like to become an actor, and I think that taking part in a drama series could be the perfect beginning of a career. It does not matter that they are crowd scenes because I like acting in any role. Additionally, it would be exciting practice for me.

b I would like to apply for this highly interesting and exciting job. Since I have always wanted to act in a film or series, this opportunity could be the perfect start of my acting career. Moreover, this job would be a great chance to get some first-hand experience in this field and gain insight into the world of acting and filming. Besides, I am visiting Innsbruck in August, and therefore I would be available at any required time.

6 **Look at the skills and qualities below and tick the ones that might promote your application. Give reasons for your choices.**

language skills | ability to work under pressure | open-minded

first aid training | IT skills | resourceful | reliable

patient | cooperative | enthusiastic | independent

work experience | decision-making skills | sense of humour

7 **Choose the better answer to content point 3:**

a Finally, I would like to enquire about details concerning the job. Could you give me the exact dates in August? Would I be acting the whole day, or would I have to stay longer in the evening? Will I earn any money for taking part? I would also like to know who will arrange my accommodation. Should I do that myself, and will you pay for it?

b Would you be so kind as to provide some details concerning the job? Firstly, it would be quite helpful to know about the exact dates in August, and also if I would have to be present all day long during this week. In addition, I would need to know whether food and accommodation will be provided. Finally, I would like to inquire if I would earn any money for taking part.

Working on reports

1 **Match the parts of the report (1–4) to the text type requirments they need to meet (a–d).**

1 subject line
2 introduction
3 body paragraphs with headings
4 conclusion

a Develop the content points (bullet points). Introduce each paragraph with a heading.
b Write a recommendation or a summary of the report, depending on the task.
c Be clear, precise and accurate about what the report is about.
d Address the *wh*-questions, such as what the report is about and why it has been written.

Layout:

Date:
From:
Subject line:
Introduction
Heading + content point
Heading + content point
Heading + content point
Conclusion

2 **Study the task below. Identify the recipient and their request.**

An educational board working with the US Embassy is preparing English language assistants for their jobs in Austria. They want to know how Austrian students benefit from working with them. Your English teacher has asked you to do a survey among students of your school and to send a report to the US Embassy.

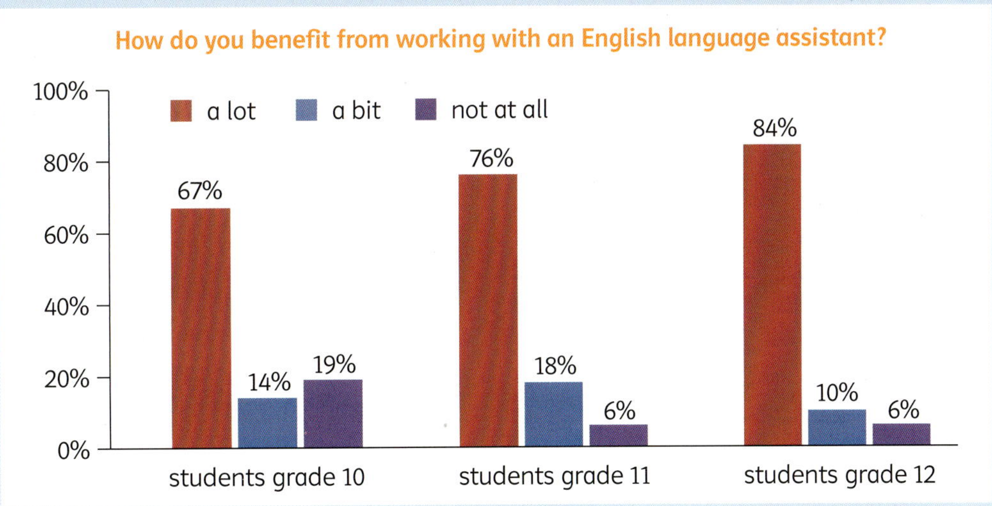

In your report you should:

- outline the results of your survey
- specify how students benefit from working with an English language assistant
- recommend additional activities for language assistants to do with students

Divide your report into sections and give them headings. Write around 400 words.

3 **Decide on the best subject line for the report.**

1 Working with an English language assistant
2 English language assistants at Austrian schools
3 Advantages of working with an English language assistant
4 Language assistants

4 **Read the introductions (1–3) and match them to the feedback below (a–c).**

1 Have you ever had a language assistant from the US at your school? Were they helpful?

2 The following report discusses to what extent Austrian students appreciate working with English language assistants and for what reasons. It also includes some further ideas on how to work with them most effectively. The insight gained is based on interviews with students from grades 10 to 12.

3 This report outlines the benefits of working with English language assistants for Austrian students. The results presented below are based on a survey which was conducted with students at Schillergymnasium Graz.

a Provides helpful information only to a limited extent, could be more detailed.
b Does not provide any information for the board of education. In addition to that, the style is not appropriate because direct questions are inappropriate in a report.
c Provides a helpful overview of what the reader can expect as well as information on the interviewees.

5 **Read the answer to content point 1 and circle the expressions used to outline the results of the survey.**

Basically, the survey shows that over two thirds of the students interviewed appreciate working with a language assistant and are aware of profiting from it. Interestingly, this figure even slightly increases with every school year, reaching nearly 85 percent in grade 12, thus indicating that the upcoming final exams might play a role here. It is then not surprising that the number of interviewees who cannot see any advantages in working with such a co-teacher decreases over the years. About one fifth of students in grade 10 can see no benefits from these lessons. This goes down to a mere six out of one hundred in grades 11 and 12.

6 **Read this section on content point 2 and circle the main argument given as well as the evidence/ examples supporting it.**

Students can profit from working with a foreign language assistant in various ways. First of all, of course, young people's language skills are improved since talking consistently to native speakers increases their confidence in how well they can express themselves. The better they get, the more opportunities will arise. For example, they might have the chance to study at any English-speaking university abroad or find a job in another country. Moreover, their increased command of the language will enable the young adults to travel more easily and to communicate even better with people from other countries.

7 **Read content point 3 again and decide what 'additional activities' implies. Choose the correct answer.**

1 all kinds of information that the assistant could offer during the lessons (on culture, politics, the American way of life, etc.)
2 activities that could be done with the language assistant outside the classroom (visit a museum, do some sports together, include the assistant in a project in another subject, etc.)

Speaking

An oral examination in English consists of two parts, an individual long turn and a paired activity. For the individual long turn, you will have a preparation time of around 10 minutes. Then you should speak for around 5 minutes. The paired activity should be spontaneous. You will have little or no time at all to prepare for it, which, however, won't matter as you will want to listen and respond to what your partner says. While the individual long turn is basically a presentation, a successful paired activity will also focus on your ability to listen carefully to your partner and to react accordingly. The paired activity should last for around 10 minutes, with each of the partners ideally filling the same amount of speaking time.

Working on individual long turns

As the individual long turn should be a presentation, it is advisable to keep eye contact with your audience and only briefly look at your notes. Never write down complete sentences during your preparation time, this will only result in you reading out sentences, which should be avoided. Instead, think of a powerful way to start and end your presentation.

An individual long turn usually opens with a prompt. This could be pictures, a chart, a cartoon, a video clip or a verbal prompt, such as a quote or part of a blog. You will be asked to start with this prompt and then deal with further content points (bullet points), which will help you to give a well-rounded presentation.

The following exercises will focus on different kinds of prompts and how to deal with them.[1]

Dealing with different kinds of prompts

1 Look at the different prompts below and decide which topic they might refer to.

A

B

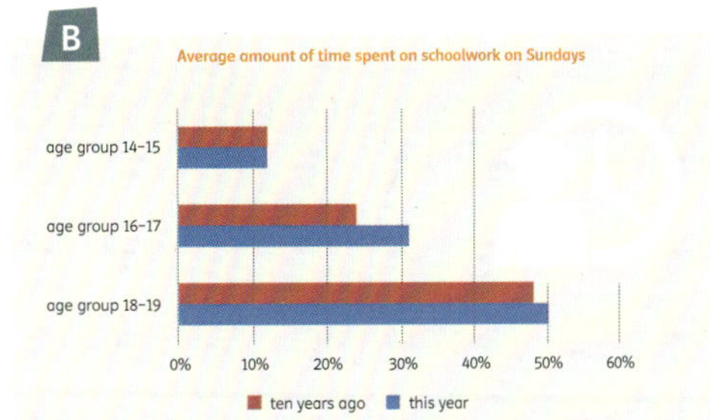

C

D

I feel sorry for the dogs

... I really can't see why people who live in small apartments in cities keep big dogs. I just feel sorry for the dogs that have to be kept on a lead whenever they go out. And the small parks around those big apartment buildings should be reserved for children, not for dogs ...

E

"Children begin by loving their parents;
as they grow older, they judge them;
sometimes they forgive them."
(*Oscar Wilde*)

[1] For how to deal with content points 2 and 3, see page 57.

2 **Study the following prompts and the suggestions about how to deal with them. Decide which ones are helpful for you. As you should speak for around 5 minutes in the individual long turn, you will have around 1½ minutes to talk about each content point. Consequently, it won't be possible to deal with all the suggestions offered here.**

TOPIC: WORK
Aspect: Different kinds of work

Give a 5-minute talk on different kinds of work.

In your talk you should:

- **discuss** the challenges the different kinds of work in the pictures might present
- …
- …

Ways to deal with the prompt

Reflect on what the function word 'discuss' requires you to do here and start with a brief description of the pictures.

1 What kind of work do the pictures show?
2 What can you tell about the people that are portrayed?

Focus on the main ideas these pictures represent.

1 What are the challenges of working outdoors/indoors?
2 Which jobs require more/less teamwork?
3 What kind of health risks/difficulties/dangers might arise when doing one of these jobs?

Ways to start your talk

Read the different ways to start your talk. One of them is less elegant. Decide which one.

1 *I would like to give a presentation on different kinds of work. Let me start by discussing the pictures. Each of them shows a different working situation …*
2 *Let me start by discussing some challenges related to different kinds of work. The pictures at hand show two types of work, namely office work, here done by a young woman sitting in front of a computer and a man, perhaps her colleague …*
3 *The first picture shows people working with computers, in the second picture, one can see people doing work on a roof.*
4 *Doing work usually involves dealing with challenges. I would like to present two different kinds of work that pose varying challenges to the people doing them …*
5 *Since my talk focuses on the topic of work, I would like to start by describing some challenges that arise when doing different kinds of work …*

TOPIC: DOMESTIC ENVIRONMENT
Aspect: Living in the city

Give a 5-minute talk on living in the city.

Alex_57
11 March, 9:15 p.m.

I feel sorry for the dogs

… I really can't see why people who live in small apartments in cities keep big dogs. I just feel sorry for the dogs that have to be kept on a lead whenever they go out. And the small parks around those big apartment buildings should be reserved for children, not for dogs …

In your talk you should:

- **comment** on the blog post above
- …
- …

Ways to deal with the prompt

Reflect on what the function word 'comment' requires you to do and start with an explanation of what the text is about.

1 What does the title tell you about the text?
2 What is the essence of the text? Use your own words as far as possible to avoid prompt lifting.
3 What is the blogger's viewpoint?
4 How could readers (people who own dogs and people who don't) respond to the blog post?

Give your opinion on the blog post.

1 Do you agree or disagree with the blogger? Support your ideas with reasons and examples.
2 Can you draw from your own experience with dogs in cities?

Ways to start your talk

Read the different ways to start your talk. One of them is less elegant. Decide which one.

1 *I would like to give a talk about a blog post.*
2 *I would like to give a talk on living in the city. Let me start by commenting on a blog post about dogs in cities.*
3 *Let me start my presentation with the question whether big dogs should be kept in small city apartments. I would like to refer to a blog post …*
4 *The topic I have chosen is domestic environment. The aspect to be discussed is living in the city. To start with, it's about dogs being kept in small city apartments.*
5 *Obviously, living in the city is not always easy. I would like to comment on a blog post about dogs in the city …*

TOPIC: EDUCATION
Aspect: Schoolwork

Give a 5-minute talk on schoolwork.

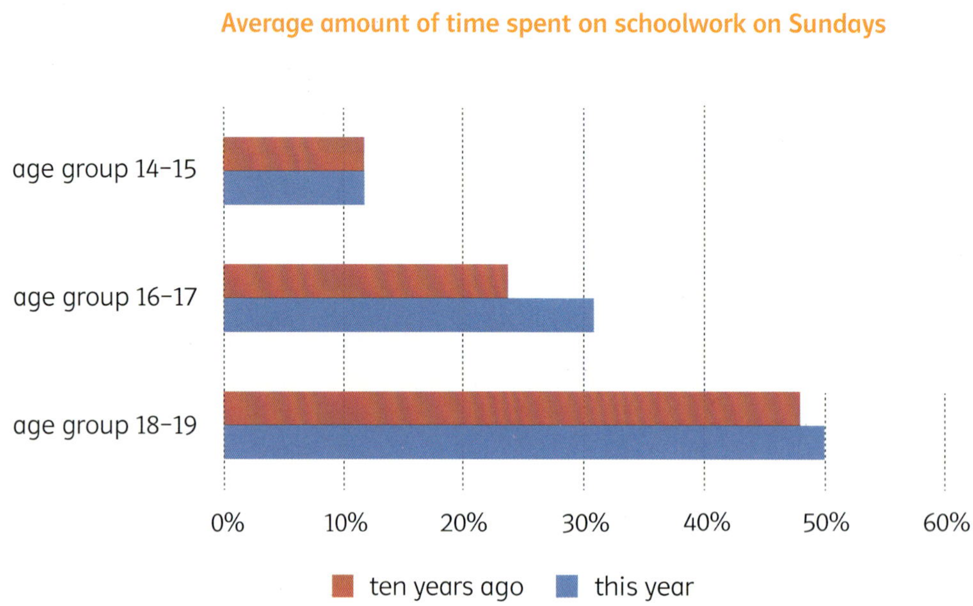

In your talk you should:

- **analyse** the results of the survey
- …
- …

Ways to deal with the prompt

Reflect on what the function word 'analyse' requires you to do here and start out with a brief description of the chart.

1 What kind of chart is it? A bar chart/pie chart/flow chart (line graph)?
2 What is it about? Which age groups/dates are referred to?
3 How do the bars in the chart differ from each other? Use quantifiers (*more than half, around one third,* etc.) when describing the chart.

Give an analysis by explaining the possible reasons for the students' answers.

1 Why does the time they spend on schoolwork increase as the students get older?
2 Why could the general workload have increased over the years?

Ways to start your talk

Read the different ways to start your talk. One of them is less elegant. Decide which one.

1 *I would like to discuss students' increasing workload over the years. Let me start by explaining what this bar chart is about.*
2 *My topic is education. I would like to start my talk with the analysis of a chart …*
3 *The topic I am going to discuss is education. In particular, I want to point out the impact of the workload students have to deal with …*
4 *I'm going to talk about the percentage of time students spend doing schoolwork on Sundays. If you look at the chart, you can clearly see …*
5 *I'm talking about a bar chart. There are three columns in the bar chart …*

TOPIC: GROWING UP
Aspect: Relationships between parents and their children

Give a 5-minute talk on growing-up.

> "Children begin by loving their parents; as they grow older, they judge them; sometimes they forgive them."
> (*Oscar Wilde*)

In your talk you should:

- **discuss** the quote
- …
- …

Ways to deal with the prompt

Reflect on what the function word 'discuss' requires you to do here and start with an interpretation of the quote.

1 What do the words 'love', 'judge', 'forgive' mean? Can you use your own words to explain the quote? Example: *Young children usually adore/admire ('love') their parents. When they turn into teenagers, they become more critical of their parents ('judge'). They start to compare them to their classmates' parents. When they become parents themselves, they might realise that their mother or father did the right thing in a certain situation ('forgive').*
2 Can you give a practical example? E.g.: *Some parents expect their children to excel at school because they did well themselves. Other parents are happy if their children just pass the year …*
3 Is the quote still relevant for young people today?

Give your personal opinion on it.

1 What do you like/dislike about the quote?
2 Why do you/don't you consider it to be interesting?
3 How do you feel about the words 'judge' and 'forgive' in connection with parents?

Ways to start your talk

Read the different ways to start your talk. One of them is less elegant. Decide which one it is.

1 *The topic I will present is 'growing up'. I would like to start with a quote by Oscar Wilde* (perhaps read out the quote). *Let me draw your attention to the words 'love', …*
2 *I'm starting my presentation on 'relationships between parents and their children' with a quote by Oscar Wilde* (perhaps read out the quote). *To put it in my own words, it means that …*
3 *Oscar Wilde was famous for his quotes. The one I want to talk about refers to 'the relationship between parents and their children'.*
4 *My topic is about a quote by Oscar Wilde. It says,* (read out the quote) …
5 *"Children begin by loving their parents." This is how Oscar Wilde starts his quote on 'growing up'. He continues with "as they grow older, …"*

Note: Many quotes are anonymous, but some can be attributed to a certain author. If you happen to know anything about the author or the author's time, you could (but you don't have to) draw on this knowledge and briefly refer to it.

TOPIC: LIFESTYLE
Aspect: Tattoos

Give a 5-minute talk on tattoos.

In your talk you should:

- **analyse** the cartoon
- …
- …

Ways to deal with the prompt

Reflect on what the function word 'analyse' requires you to do here and start with a brief description of the cartoon.

1. What is the setting of the cartoon?
2. How many people are shown? What are they doing?
3. How does the cartoonist exaggerate in his portrayal of the people/situations?
4. What does the text say? How does it relate to the picture?

Point out the main idea of the cartoon.

1. What (social/political/economic …) issue(s) does it address?
2. What makes the cartoon effective?
3. Who is the intended audience? What might their reaction be?
4. Is the cartoon successful in conveying the cartoonist's message?
5. Is the cartoon ambiguous in any way? Would different people interpret it differently?

Ways to start your talk

Read the different ways to start your talk. One of them is less elegant. Decide which one.

1. *The topic I would like to discuss is lifestyle, in particular, getting tattoos and having them removed. Let me briefly describe the cartoon at hand …*
2. *I would like to start my presentation by analysing a cartoon. It shows some young people who intend to get a tattoo and some older people who want to get rid of their tattoos for a much higher price.*
3. *Let me start my talk by giving a short analysis of a cartoon about tattoos.*
4. *I can see some people going into a tattoo studio. The studio on the left says "Tattoos for $50", …*
5. *The cartoon depicts two tattoo parlours. In one parlour you can get a tattoo, in the other one you can have it removed.*

Dealing with content points 2 and 3 and ending your individual long turn

Dealing well with the prompt can be a powerful introduction to your talk. However, keep in mind that addressing and expanding content points two and three is just as important. So use your preparation time wisely and don't spend all the time you have on the prompt.

Ways to prepare for content points 2 and 3

1 **Brainstorm ideas** and **make notes**. Mark your ideas as more or less important for your talk. If necessary, find advantages and disadvantages of the issues at hand. Draw mind maps with the main idea in the middle and supporting arguments, explanations and examples around it. Again, never write down complete sentences.
2 Consider the **function words**. For instance, do you have to explain something, or do you have to make a recommendation? Do you have to speculate about something, or do you have to convince or persuade your listeners?
3 The most important thing is that you support whatever you intend to say with **good reasons and examples**. Remember the **PEEL strategy** (**p**oint – **e**vidence/example – **e**xplanation – **l**ink to the original idea).
4 When talking about the **content points**, remember that you have **around 1½ minutes for each of them**. If possible, try to follow the order of the content points. Sometimes, however, it may make sense to come back to a previous content point, especially if the prompt (one of the pictures, the chart, the quote) is of special relevance to the following content point(s).

Ways to move from one content point to the next

Read the suggestions below. Two of them are less elegant. Decide which ones.

1 *Now, let me continue with another aspect of the topic* (rephrase the content point).
2 *The picture on the left/right leads me to another interesting point* (read/rephrase the content point).
3 *Now, I want to talk about the second bullet point …*
4 *I'd now like to present a different angle on the topic. Namely, how … can be improved/solved/ changed …*
5 *Finally, I would like to highly recommend … If you …, you will certainly notice …*
6 *To conclude/Last but not least, I would like to draw your attention to …*
7 *The last bullet point says* (read out the bullet point) …
8 *People often wonder why … I can give you the answer to it.*
9 *Let me go back to what I said before about … I would like to add …*

Ways to end an individual long turn successfully

Find a compelling way to end your presentation. Look at the examples below. Two of them are less elegant. Decide which ones.

1 *This was my presentation on … I hope you liked it.*
2 *Coming to the end of my presentation, I would like to stress/underline …*
3 *All things considered, the drawbacks outweigh the benefits for …*
4 *Allow me to add my opinion on … as a conclusion (to my talk).*
5 *Finally, I would like to draw your attention again to …*
6 *Let me round up my presentation by focusing again on what I have said before …*
7 *I think this is all I can say …*
8 *At the end of my talk, I would like to draw your attention again to …*

Practising individual long turns

1 Prepare for around 10 minutes. Brainstorm ideas and make notes. Then compare your ideas with the suggestions on the next page.

TOPIC: TRAVELLING
Aspect: Different holiday types

Give a 5-minute talk on different types of holiday.

In your talk you should:

- **compare** the different types of holiday as shown in the pictures
- **speculate** about what makes people book an adventure holiday
- **argue** that spending a holiday in one's own country might be a good idea

Notes:

Tips for what you could say

content point 1

- ***compare*** *the different types of holiday as shown in the pictures*

Introduction: Briefly refer to any similarities between the pictures: targeted at holiday makers who want something special

Main aspect: Focus on the main differences between the holiday pictures:

- **Rock climbing:** active holiday, can be done individually or as part of an organised tour, special gear and personal fitness needed, possibly risky, dependent on weather conditions, possible destinations Austria/ Switzerland, etc.
- **Safari:** passive enjoyment, organised tour, probably costly, not really environmentally friendly (disturbs animals, long-haul flights), no special gear/personal fitness needed, possible destination Africa, etc.
- **Ice hotel:** exclusive, unique winter holiday, unusual environment, often booked as an individual holiday, expensive, unusual place to sleep, relatively cold interior, not suitable for everyone, potential health risks, possible destinations Sweden/Iceland, etc.

content point 2

- ***speculate*** *about what makes people book an adventure holiday*

Possible ideas: Interested in other cultures? Widen one's horizons? Have a thrill-seeking personality? Try something new? Impress friends? Looking for a challenge? Need a workout? Test your limits? Seek something exclusive and unique?

→ Choose the most likely ideas and give reasons for them (PEEL), e.g.:
Many holidaymakers simply want to impress their friends. They want to tell stories about roaring lions and dangerous encounters, …

content point 3

- ***argue*** *that spending a holiday in one's own country might be a good idea*

Possible ideas: save money, get to know one's country better, see other parts of your country, support your country's tourism industry, good for the environment, no extra vaccinations/ malaria tablets necessary, fewer health risks, familiar language/food, etc.

→ Choose the most likely ideas and give reasons for them (PEEL), e.g.:
A really convincing argument why people should spend their holiday in their own country would be that they could actually get to know it better. They could learn about its past by visiting historical sights, …

2 Read the task below and prepare for around 10 minutes brainstorming ideas and making notes. Then do the task and record it. Listen to it and tick off the questions in the feedback grid below.

TOPIC: ENVIRONMENTAL ISSUES
Aspect: Clean water/preserving nature

Give a 5-minute talk on environmental issues.

In your talk you should:

- **contrast** the situations shown in the pictures
- **discuss** the importance of clean water for all living beings
- **suggest** how to preserve nature for future generations

Did you ...	yes	yes, somewhat	very little	no
1 introduce the topic?				
2 give a very brief description of the pictures? (content point 1)				
3 focus on the contrasting situations? (cp 1)				
4 move elegantly from content point 1 to content point 2?				
5 give good reasons with supporting/relevant details when talking about the importance of clean water? (cp 2)				
6 include all living beings? (cp 2)				
7 move elegantly from content point 2 to content point 3?				
8 provide relevant evidence/examples/reasons when suggesting how to preserve nature for future generations? (cp 3)				
9 conclude your talk in a compelling way?				
10 speak for around 5 minutes?				

Working on and practising paired activities

The information and exercises below will focus on task achievement and interaction, which are common challenges when doing a paired activity.

Task achievement

In a paired activity, you will have to consider the situational context and content points that you need to discuss. The situational context addresses *wh*-questions: What will you have to discuss, why, and what is the expected outcome of your discussion?

Dealing with situational contexts

1 **Answer these questions for each of the following tasks.**

1 What is the **setting** of your task?
2 What is the **topic/aspect** of your discussion? What do you have to/will you talk about?
3 What is the **aim** of your discussion? What should you and your partner have decided at the end?

A Sports

An international organisation working with the IOC[2] has invited you to give a presentation on aspects of sports young people might be interested in.

You have 10 minutes to discuss with a partner which aspects of sports you might want to talk about. Discuss the suggestions below and agree on two.

Setting:

Topic + aspect:

Aim:

B Domestic environment/housing

You and your partner are looking for suitable student accommodation in a mid-sized town in the UK.

You have 10 minutes to discuss which of the features below are important for you when choosing an area to live in. Rank them according to their importance from 1 (most important) to 5 (least important).

Setting:

Topic + aspect:

Aim:

C Intercultural issues

An international committee working with the Austrian government is discussing whether young Austrians should be encouraged to take a gap year in a developing country. You have been asked to give your opinion on this matter.

You have 10 minutes to discuss your recommendations with a partner. Consider the possible opportunities and challenges below and make a clear recommendation.

Setting:

Topic + aspect:

Aim:

[2] **IOC:** (*abbr. for*) International Olympic Committee

Dealing with the content points

Both partners are required to address and expand each of the content points and support what they are saying with relevant details, such as evidence/examples and reasons. Depending on the task, they should discuss:

- possible pros/opportunities/benefits as well as cons/challenges/obstacles
- which of them are more/less relevant for your final agreement/decision/recommendation

2 **Match the content points below to the situational contexts from above.**

Task: ______	Task: ______	Task: ______
▪ food ▪ language ▪ daily routines ▪ traditions ▪ climate	▪ national athletes as role models ▪ sports education in school ▪ media coverage of sports events ▪ current fitness crazes ▪ the business side of sports	▪ public transport ▪ restaurants ▪ parks ▪ shopping facilities ▪ entertainment options

3 **Think of possible pros and cons etc. for each of these content points and decide which of them you would consider to be important for your final suggestion.**

4 **You will most likely have to discuss five options. However, some tasks might offer four or five options *and* require you to add your own idea/suggestion. For each of the three tasks above, find another option which you might like to discuss.**

▪ ______	▪ ______	▪ ______

Interaction

Successful interaction is natural and spontaneous. It includes initiating and maintaining the discussion, negotiating and interrupting appropriately and distributing the speaking time equally.

Tips for successful interaction

5 **Cross out the four tips that are not advisable for successful interaction.**

1 Listen carefully to what your partner says.
2 Interrupt your partner politely to express your view if necessary.
3 Take notes while your partner is speaking.
4 Invite your partner to express his/her opinion.
5 Let your partner know that you understand what he/she says.
6 Look at the interlocutor while listening to your partner.
7 Make sure your partner understands what you want to say.
8 Interview your partner.
9 Make use of body language (e.g. nodding, smiling, gestures) to show your partner that you are listening.
10 Be polite when disagreeing with your partner.
11 Pick up on your partner's ideas.
12 Dominate the discussion.

Ways to interact in a paired activity

6 **Study the possible ways to interact (1–30), then match them to the explanations (a–g). There may be more than one correct answer.**

a you fully or partly disagree with your partner
b you want to buy time
c you want to consider another aspect/content point
d you don't have an opinion on something
e you don't know anything about an issue
f you want to make sure you have understood correctly
g you want to interrupt your partner politely

1 *Absolutely/Exactly.* a
2 *Let me add something here.*
3 *Are you saying that …?*
4 *Well, perhaps we can take a look at …*
5 *I guess you're quite right.*
6 *Give me a second.*
7 *I'm not sure I can agree.*
8 *I can't really go along with that.*
9 *I don't have any strong feelings either way.*
10 *I have no idea/clue.*
11 *Really? I'd rather believe …*
12 *Now, if we consider another aspect …*
13 *I suppose so.*
14 *Hold on, do you really believe that …?*
15 *Well, let me think …*
16 *You've got a point there.*
17 *That's exactly what I wanted to say.*
18 *Can I stop you there for a moment?*
19 *I've been wondering about that too.*
20 *It doesn't make any difference to me.*
21 *To be honest, that's not how I see it.*
22 *Do you mind if I come in here?*
23 *I'm with you on that …*
24 *So, what you mean is …*
25 *I've never given it much thought.*
26 *That's a good question.*
27 *I couldn't agree with you more.*
28 *Beats me.*
29 *Not necessarily.*
30 *Another aspect that might influence …*

Ways to begin and end a discussion

Since you should try to share the speaking time equally between you, one student could start the discussion and the other could conclude it. Depending on the nature of the discussion, beginnings and endings will be different.

7 **Decide which of the following sentences are beginnings (B) and which ones are endings (E). One of them is less elegant. Decide which one it is.**

1 *Right. The task at hand is to make a recommendation on … How can we go about it? Do you have an idea?* B
2 *Well, after considering all options, we have decided on … as our first choice.*
3 *I think it's a great opportunity to talk about … at this conference. I would like to start discussing … if you don't mind.*
4 *Now we have discussed several options …, but we agree to disagree on …*
5 *I'm glad we could finally agree on … That means, we can present … to the committee.*
6 *Would you like to start the discussion?*
7 *Let me summarise what we have said so far …*
8 *All right. I guess we have come to a final decision. For the issue at hand, … is most important, followed by …*
9 *This is our present situation. We have been invited … and we need to discuss … and agree on the two most/least important aspects. Let me start with …*
10 *Let me conclude what we've agreed on. We have decided to disregard … and … Therefore, we can agree on … and …*

8 **Now find a partner and practise the paired activities on pages 61/62.**

Texts

4/5 https://www.survivalinternational.org/articles/3197-human-safaris-when-does-tourism-become-unethical; **6/7** Chris Telden, '10 Best Science Fiction Short Stories of All Time: From the Golden Age to the Modern Era', *HobbyLark*, 15 November 2019, https://hobbylark.com/fandoms/Best-Science-Fiction-Short-Story (slightly adapted); **8/9** Tom Crouch, '1908: The Year the Airplane Went Public', *airspacemag.com*, 28 August 2008, https://www.airspacemag.com/history-of-flight/1908-the-year-the-airplane-went-public-8791602/ (slightly adapted); **10/11** *The Economist*, Print edition, 4 May 2019, https://www.economist.com/business/2019/05/02/struggling-with-style (slightly adapted); **12/13** Magda Origjanska, 'The history of the gymnasium: from a school for naked exercise to wellness empire', 1 December 2017, https://www.thevintagenews.com/2017/12/01/history-of-the-gymnasium-2/; **14/15** *The Economist*, Print edition, 12 May 2018, https://www.economist.com/books-and-arts/2018/05/10/to-master-a-language-start-learning-it-early (slightly adapted); **24** Shelley Metcalfe, 'Online advertising: Why we need to educate young people', *The Digital Life Skills Company*, 29 January 2019, https://www.digitallifeskills.org.uk/spotting_advertsing_online_educate_young_people/

Pictures

4 FG Trade / Getty Images; **6** Colourbox.com; **8** peterspiro / Getty Images; **10** PeopleImages / Getty Images; **12** CasarsaGuru / Getty Images; **14** btrenkel / iStockphoto.com; **17** Ingram Publishing / Thinkstock; **18** MEV-Verlag, Germany; **20** rrodrickbeiler / Getty Images; **21** RobChristiaans / Thinkstock; **22** Riccardo Lennart Niels Mayer / Thinkstock; **24** oneblink-cj / Getty Images - iStockphoto; **26** denis_pc / Getty Images - iStockphoto; **27** nimis69 / Getty Images - iStockphoto; **28** Hemera Technologies - AbleStock.com / Thinkstock; **29** Library of Congress / Everett Collection / picturedesk.com; **31** Capuski / Getty Images; **33** Okea / iStockphoto.com; **35.1** 4x6 / Getty Images - iStockphoto; **35.2** herraez / Getty Images; **36** jevelin / Getty Images - iStockphoto; **37** sturti / Getty Images - iStockphoto; **39** Tom Mc Nemar / Fotolia; **40** sturti / iStockphoto.com; **41** kali9 / Getty Images; **42** a_namenko / Getty Images - iStockphoto; **43** Ruth Black / Fotolia; **46** Natalya Aleksakhina / Thinkstock; **50** DGLimages / Getty Images - iStockphoto; **51.1** deimagine / Getty Images; **51.2** John McPherson / Cartoonstock; **52.1** PeopleImages / Getty Images; **52.2** TerryJ / Getty Images - iStockphoto; **53** FluxFactory / Getty Images - iStockphoto; **56.1** John McPherson / Cartoonstock; **56.2** Evgeniy Kuznetsov / Getty Images - iStockphoto; **58.1** deimagine / Getty Images; **58.2** pierivb / Getty Images - iStockphoto; **58.3** icehotel.com / Action Press / picturedesk.com; **60.1** JackF / Getty Images - iStockphoto; **60.2** vitranc / Getty Images; **62** PIKSEL / Getty Images - iStockphoto; **63** AaronAmat / Getty Images - iStockphoto